The Alchemy of Lightness

Contents

chapter 5: change our consciousness to change our riding   97

chapter 6 – living in lightness   115

an end and a beginning   131

Preface: A Zen Story

Art by Lauren Schultz based on a sequence of ten illustrations "Taming the Wild Ox," depicting the levels of realization in the search for spiritual illumination by Zen Master Kakuan, China, twelfth century. The horse represents one's true nature—the "emptiness of consciousness," a presence in an infinite field of awareness, knowingness, and oneness... spiritual awakening. The ten illustrations depict progressive steps of awareness leading ever closer to enlightenment.

The horse (my true nature) has never been lost, so why do I search? In confusion I lose even the smallest signs of my true nature, my existence.

After a long search I begin to understand that I have not lost anything and I discover the tracks (signs) of my true nature, the existence of my true self.

I perceive the horse. I perceive that he is not apart from (my) self.

My true nature dwelt in the wilderness a long time. The mind is stubborn and unbridled, distracted and wandering. I must catch my true nature, my understanding of consciousness.

Discipline and practice are needed to tame the wandering and distraction of my consciousness (true nature). There is no room for doubt.

After the struggle I sit astride my horse (my true nature), and return to my life. Onward I go, observing all, maintaining discipline and practice.

I reach my home, in serenity. My horse can rest. My true nature is transcended. I have no need of strong measures or force, although my discipline and practice remains.

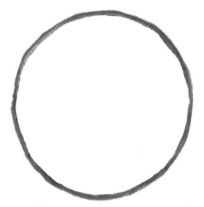

Horse and self have transcended, merging in "no-thing-ness"—emptiness of consciousness, presence without qualities, no craving, no attachment, no desire. The understanding of the vastness of the universe brings silence and peace in humility. There is no limitation.

From the beginning, my true nature was evident. In silence I see integration and disintegration. I see that which is creating and that which is destroying.

Everywhere I look I see enlightenment. I seek no honor or acknowledgement. I seek to share the existence of my true nature.

To the Reader

This text was written collaboratively and with one focus, and therefore a singular voice. My coauthor Dominique Barbier, a renowned horseman and clinician, has shared his insights and love for the horse with the world for over 40 years. Because of this, as a horse trainer, I agreed to collaborate on this project as it is in direct alignment with aspects of riding and living closest to my heart. Exploring how we can facilitate the communion between horse and human, two animals, resulted in dialogues, which birthed this book. While we had initially started with an outline and a general blueprint of the content, it was the meandering of our discussions that yielded the depth and honesty you will find in its pages. And it is this synergy of mind and soul between two people that opens the door to explaining the synergy of mind and soul that we seek with our horses.

Many people require "proof" in order to develop a belief or faith in the existence of something. Therefore, the pages ahead include mention of recent scientific findings meant only as an introduction to one way we can explain complex phenomena, such as telepathy, psychic connection, and interconnectedness. In recent years, advances in the sciences, especially in the field of quantum physics, give us valuable insight into concepts critical in the communion between animals. Recent experiments conducted and elucidated by scientific writers such as Dr. Bruce Lipton (*The Biology of Belief*); Lynne McTaggart (*The Field*); and Gregg Braden (*The Divine Matrix*), to name a few, allow us to begin to explain and teach what has eluded many, and appeared to come naturally or by sheer magic to some.

In science, what is accepted as truth quickly becomes obsolete as new findings and methodologies continue to expand our understanding. People often take scientific revelations and weight them as more valuable or as truth when in fact they are transient, malleable, and forever evolving. With this in mind, scientific notes included in this book are not meant to be a concrete dictation but merely an invitation to encourage the reader to continue to be open to the great possibilities of how we can be present and be "one" with our horse.

Coincidently, in recent travels to Spain I became acquainted with Salvador Dali's surrealist painting "Transparent Horse" (*jinete transparente. Figura ecuestre molecular—1952*), which eloquently captures the concepts in this book. The painting depicts the molecules that link us together, human and horse, and it is this web of interconnectedness that explains the alchemic process involved in creating lightness. What a miracle to have this image predict, more than 50 years before now, the science in the art of equitation. And, as this book also intends to be, Dali's painting is an invitation to a personal journey to elevate our horsemanship and thereby our state of being.

It is my hope that, just like Salvador Dali's painting, this book speaks to you, and that its contents remain relevant many years from now—elegant and timeless.

Dr. Maria Katsamanis

how this book came to be

We meet and unite with other human beings in life in ways not unlike we meet and unite with horses. In my travels and teaching, I am honored to have the opportunity to share my ideas with others, and at the same time be open to their own questions, thoughts, and theories. When horsewoman and academic Dr. Maria Katsamanis offered her knowledge of the world of science, and outlined the parallels new research offers my own spiritual and instinctual leanings as an *écuyer*, I was excited, as was she, about the possibilities—the proverbial doors it opened to better understanding how we become one with a horse.

It would be strange for a text meant to unite to read as disparate parts. It would separate us from our goal of communion if this book did not fully integrate my philosophy with the information Dr. Katsamanis provides. Therefore, the pages that follow are the result of questions asked and answers given, and are evidence of my personal experience with horses and Dr. Katsamanis' personal experience with science. Yet they are also proof of a kind of, you could say, "alchemical transformation" or *transmutation*: Our two voices, our two areas of expertise, our two loves for the horse and all he represents, have joined and become something different—one message of *who* we can be, *how* we can be, and *what* we can ultimately become... something beautiful...something *golden*.

Amities,
D. Barbier

Introduction

a time of change

A recent shift in world consciousness is responsible
for a heightened awareness and a hunger for greater understanding of many aspects of our existence.
Universal dissatisfaction with current standards
that inhibit our relationship potential with the horse
compels some to seek answers and understand the
true essence of *légèreté*—"lightness"—for the infinite
possibilities it can reveal in our understanding of the
horse, of ourselves, and of our world. Thus begins the
quest to consider what lightness is, how to get it and
maintain it, and what changes it inspires.

"It is the time to leave the Flatland of conscienceless and unconscious pursuits. It is time to move on to something greater and more noble."

David G. Yurth, PhD

to preserve classical principles

Riding is an *equestrian art*, which means that it can be elevated to whatever we want it to be. We would expect that anyone involved with a horse is able to feel that artistic and spiritual dimension. It is very sad that most people have no awareness that it even exists.

With this book I want to demonstrate that there is more to riding than sitting on the horse. My vision is to show that it is a creative art that can be developed and enjoyed and shared. For riding to emerge as "something more," the horse must be respected and his well-being held in high regard. It is necessary, then, to put your equine partner in a physical and mental position where he can express himself. That is of primary importance.

Knowledge of the core principles of the "Classical School" of training philosophy has been lost, and consequently, the very essence of dressage has been challenged. Many authentic *écuyers* (riders) have, in their lifetime, failed to translate the intricacies of their own riding into a language from which others can learn. Many have flirted with the manner of fame brought only by sport dressage competition. Many have "sold their soul," so to speak. Very few know the classical principles or defend them, as they are not very popular in our modern society of instant gratification.

For many decades, trainers (including myself) have not helped this matter—the *secret de rigueur* (strict secret) meant we kept our methods to ourselves like well-guarded recipes. But now there is an accelerated urgency to make the classical principles clearer and more accessible. The situation is so dramatic that we risk losing the very meaning of dressage.

Through this book, I intend to demystify the idea of true French lightness (*la belle légèreté à la française*) and examine how this elusive "oneness" with a horse originates through a means I describe as "Molecular Equitation" (*L'Equitation Moleculaire*). It is the scientific study of the interplay of mechanisms put in motion when man and horse meet, communicate, and

There is a transformation that occurs when the human is in contact with the animal. This molecular transformation brings a change in consciousness that we are going to study. This is a transmutation.

ultimately become one. Through the principles of Molecular Equitation, I also will discuss the definition of lightness by illustrating how the flow of molecules, in time and space, generate and enhance the communication between the horse and the rider. Understanding *how* lightness is generated is examined using the simple and elegant basics of the universe: atoms and molecules, which exist all around us. Scientific findings and theoretical underpinnings allow us to better understand *how* that process occurs—and how to harness it.

When I wrote the following in French, I "found" the theme of this book: *Il y a une transformation du l'être humain au contact de l'animal. C'est cette transformation moleculaire qui entraine un changement de conscience que nous allons étudier. C'est une transmutation.* This translates to, "There is a transformation that occurs when the human is in contact with the animal. This molecular transformation brings a change in consciousness that we are going to study. This is a transmutation."

Molecular Equitation approaches riding in the modern day just as François Baucher looked at riding differently in the mid-1800s. At that time, Baucher recognized a change in the nature of horses. The Thoroughbred became *à la mode* (in fashion) overnight and transformed the art of riding because he was a very different style of horse—with his racing qualities came a new set of challenges, both physical and mental.

Now in this new age, our personal goals are evolving: Not only do we wish to *look* good, we also want to *feel* good, to take care of our nutrition, to be mindful of our general wellness. In the same way, we want to take care of our equine companion. The horse's welfare—in body and mind—has become a very important factor in our relationship with him. We want to better understand biomechanical aspects of riding, as well as the mental communication that can develop between horse and human. Like Baucher, we want to have a concrete and scientific understanding of the much sought-after quality of "oneness."

To explain what occurs between horse and human, we now have the ability to measure and quantify certain phenomena that a very few years ago were considered paranormal—that is, not serious, even illegitimate. Some of these exist as "possibilities" but have not yet been scientifically proven. They include, but are not limited to, the molecular changes resulting from thoughts and feelings[1]; the effects of feeling on water crystals[2]; the role of DNA in our communion with others[3, 4]; the power of breath work and yoga; and the impact of harnessing vibrational frequencies and quantum physics.[1, 3, 5-11]

For example, we want to understand *why* people "feel better" around horses. What is the healing process: both healing *of* the horse and healing *from* the horse? What occurs during focused visualization and how does forming a mental image manifest as vibrations and frequencies? Are these molecular processes or not? What is it that happens in the meditative space that exists when "two become one"—where everything works?

The horse is an instrument of molecular change because he is the creator of a new consciousness. In order to gain his trust, we must give away complete control. If we give the horse control, he gives us back this consciousness. The horse is a vehicle to enlightenment.

beyond xenophon, baucher, la guérinière, and oliveira

In my previous book, *Dressage for the New Age*, I introduced French classical principles with a key focus on the mental component of riding. An emphasis on this mental element has been my life's work, and it is apparent in both my teaching and my riding. Although many notable masters over the centuries have acknowledged the existence of a mental side to equestrian pursuits, the physical part has long received more attention. Therefore, it is my primary goal to reinforce the importance of understanding and honing the mental component.

My second objective is to heighten awareness of the horse's comfort or lack thereof. It is of such consequence that any exercise likely to cause him physical or mental distress should be discontinued. The combination of his physical and mental comfort allows for the spiritual experiences that draw us to horses in the first place. It is this draw, and my own great love for them, that continues to inspire me to create and quantify the idea of "oneness" in the saddle.

The following pages draw from various researchers and authors whose careers have focused on understanding such constructs as consciousness, interbeing (the idea there is not independent self), intuition, and the power of emotions. It references books, such as *The Divine Matrix*[4] by Gregg Braden, that document our ability to harness energy. Braden's research, in particular, suggests that a field of energy connects us to one another. This field mirrors our beliefs, and we communicate with it via what is known as "the language of emotion." As a result, it empowers us to be active "creators" in the world around us, meaning we have the ability to determine the success of our relationships and connections with other people, our horses, and the greater cosmos.

"The horse is already trained. He is teaching you the way he wants to be ridden."

Mestre Nuno Oliveira

Know that this book is not intended to elaborate on the history or details of science, nor explain in depth the principles of "new physics." It is, however, meant to include scientific findings that offer insight into the possibilities that our experiences with horses have a quantifiable explanation. As is the case with scientific findings, conclusions are finite for our understanding and the methods of evaluation are ever-changing. Theories evolve and findings once deemed of interest are disproved.

In contrast, the classical principles of riding endure.

chapter 1

The Science in the Art of Equitation

why science is important to riding at this time

It was in the quest to understand better what exists in our relationship with the horse that my search began for information on the alchemic phenomenon that occurs when we experience oneness with a horse. There are people who will not even look at something if it is not scientifically proven, as if it does not exist. And there are many who doubt a thing's very existence when it is not "concrete." But what if we are able to actually define the mechanisms of what happens between a man and a horse and prove that there is definitely something at work?

There is, in fact, a whole array of what used to be defined as "paranormal phenomena" that has now, more and more, become accepted and considered "mainstream." The addition of a "scientific lens" to our personal experience with our horses becomes yet another way for us to integrate key ingredients and advance our consciousness as riders and humans to the next level. Many discoveries emerging from the scientific community are directly relevant to our interaction with our animals and provide a great complement to what I originally introduced to the equestrian community—and what has become my life's passion.

The addition of a "scientific lens" to our personal experience with our horses becomes yet another way for us to integrate key ingredients and advance our consciousness as riders and humans to the next level.

the scientific story

At the very frontier of scientific thought, new ideas are emerging that challenge everything we believe about how our world works and our relationship with ourselves and other living beings. For decades, respected scientists in a variety of disciplines all over the world have been carrying out well-designed experiments whose results fly in the face of current biology and physics. Together, these studies offer information about the central organizing force governing our bodies and the rest of the cosmos.

What they have discovered is nothing less than astonishing. At our most elemental, we are not a chemical reaction, but an energetic charge. Human beings and all other living things are linked and connected in a pulsating "field" of energy, which is the central engine in the relationship between the mind and the world with which it must interact.[4, 12-14]

what happens between horse and human on a molecular level

Our relationships with animals and the molecular interactions that happen from them to us, and from us to them, enrich all the other relationships we have. These processes—which we are often not conscious

the alchemy of lightness

of—are actually intermolecular exchanges of energy. These intermolecular energy exchanges create change, a transmutation—the action of changing or the state of being changed into another form. In other words, it is this energy exchange that allows for *molecular change*.

The molecular process that would allow for "oneness" with another being necessitates having an openness of mind and a "childlike" imagination willing to accept the invitation to explore the endless possibilities that can exist between a human and an animal. This is also an invitation to entertain the idea that there is a different way of training, a different way of being with the horse. The result is nothing short of an alchemical process that creates change on a molecular level. We have to be conscious of the fact that how we think impacts how we interact with the horse, how we communicate with him.

"Although we perceive science as an ultimate truth, science is finally just a story, told in installments. If we are in constant and instantaneous dialogue with our environment, if all the information from the cosmos flows through our pores at every moment, then our current notion of our human potential is only a glimmer of what it should be."

Lynne McTaggart, Author of *The Field*

who we are, not what we do

The more self-disciplined we are, the more conscious we are of our body because our mind is more "available" and compassionate, and the better prepared we are to be received by the horse. The more we are aware of *who we are*, the better the chances that any situation can be dealt with. If we are calm and centered, the horse will likely pass through resistance or disturbance much more easily. He will happily partner with us. The horse is ready for us. His state is pure. We have to preserve that purity of feeling by being as "clean" as we can for him. Let me explain what I mean by "clean."

The horse is ready for us.
His state is pure.

When you first connect with a horse, something happens. In the initial contact, there is a lot of communication; the *energy exchange* I mentioned on p. 9 occurs. When entering the stable or going to the paddock, your first visual contact with the horse is the beginning of your relationship with him. Make sure you are prepared, meaning you have left the frustration and complications of your daily life behind you. Bring who you really are, clear and open. Welcome him; breathe and smile.

As mentioned, this first connection starts the relationship; after that, you can decide what shape the relationship will take: Will it simply be a physical one, or will it be more sophisticated? Slow down your breath, your vibration; breathe out; be mindful of your movement around your horse. Then *be* the best you can: Your tact, your sensibility, your love will be ready to produce magic. This is the start of making your intermolecular energy exchange, and thereby *molecular change*, a conscious one.

molecules as vehicles of information transfer between two beings

So how does the intermolecular energy exchange we have mentioned occur? To understand the process, we must look at the basic elements that make up all living beings. These invisible particles explain how our encounters with other living beings are, quite simply, exchanges of *energy*. The *charge* of the electrical exchange dictates how we feel and what transpires as a result.

However, an intermolecular exchange is nothing without its key component: the *molecule*. Molecules are the small particles that make up all living and nonliving things. They consist of even tinier particles, called *atoms*, which in turn subsist of *subatomic* particles that dictate how the atom works. Molecules comprise the cells of our body and constitute how *we* work.

What's so special about the molecules in our body and those in other living things? Each molecule has a unique shape that allows it to interact with other molecules. These interactions between molecules let us and other living things move, sense, and reproduce, to name just a few activities necessary to maintaining life. Molecules interact via forces of attraction that dictate the strength of the bonds between them.

Recent scientific discoveries, discussed in more detail in the chapters ahead, can serve as yet another window to explore what happens in our experience with horses on a molecular level.[15-17] Quantum physics has been largely successful in describing the behavior of things that are smaller than the atom—so successful, in fact, that a set of "rules" has been created to describe what we can expect to happen in this "invisible" world.

the web of connection

New discoveries about the mutable nature of molecules and atoms lend more weight to the idea that *consciousness* (awareness, sense of self) may be central in shaping our experience with horses. Dozens of scientists[13, 18-21] have documented the existence of something referred to as the "vast quantum web" of connection. The existence of a "web" that connects us, molecule to molecule, begins to explain the idea of how the exchange of energy, or information transfer, occurs between living beings. In fact, information between two living beings is conveyed much faster than previously thought. It is through what is called the *torsion field* that the information transfer rate is thought by some to be at least 10^9 times faster than the speed of light. [22-26, 27] Gregg Braden, author of *The Divine Matrix*, writes, "From the DNA of our bodies to the atoms of everything else, things in nature appear to share information more rapidly than Albert Einstein predicted anything could ever travel—faster than the speed of light. In some experiments, data has even arrived at its destination *before* it has left its place of origin."

I will elaborate on how some of these scientific findings explain our connection to our horses, to our "dream ride," and to ourselves, in the chapters ahead.

the dna code of communication

So how does our DNA—the molecule that encodes the genetic instructions for development and functioning in all living organisms—work in the creation of this molecule-to-molecule communication? How is it linked to our potential for a deep connection to our horses? How is our DNA linked to consciousness? Research has produced evidence suggesting that consciousness is the result of the brain and DNA acting as transducers—transmuting, receiving from, and ultimately translating information from the quantum "field" (that web of connection I mentioned above).[28]

Science can explain how when we touch another person or animal, a trace of our DNA stays with the other person or animal in the skin cells that

The problem is that we think we are human but we always are in between...

part animal, part human, part God.

we leave behind—and vice versa. Does that imply that we continue to be linked to those we touch as long as DNA in the cells we share is alive? If so, what is the depth of that connection? Research suggests that the link exists. The quality of the connection, however, appears to be determined by how conscious we are of its existence—in other words, do we acknowledge and nurture it rather than deny or ignore it?

the molecules of emotion

Another ingredient in the quantum web of connection is *emotion*. The role that emotion plays in the processes of thought, memory, and human consciousness is key. Emotions become the elixir that fast-tracks and enhances our experiences, further explaining how we commune with our environment and other living beings.

Understanding the basic framework of how emotions are generated in the system provides a brief window of clarity in the interplay between molecules, energy, and their role in consciousness. Emotions are part of the mechanisms and behavior of more than 60 different amino-acid-based molecules known as *neuropeptides*, which are responsible for communicating information throughout the human body and influencing the brain in certain ways. Dr. Candace Pert,[30] a researcher interested in the area of consciousness, discovered that emotional states are created in the body by the release of chemicals called *endorphins* (internally produced morphines—"feel good" molecules). These chemicals, and others like them, are involved in what Dr. Pert deemed "a psychosomatic communication network," illustrating that information flows continuously through the body, carried by the neuropeptide molecules—biochemical units of emotion. They regulate and actually "create" the emotions we feel.

We now understand, via advances in imaging technologies such as Positron Emission Tomography (PET) and functional Magnetic Resonance Imaging (fMRI), the inner workings of the brain as we emote, think, and behave. For example, emotions such as fear and anger are associated with consistent and predicable brain wave patterns.[31] Dr. Bruce Lipton (author of *The Biology of Belief*)[1] possesses a deep understanding of cell biology (he holds a doctorate in Developmental Cell Biology from the University of Virginia) and in his writings suggests that our bodies can be *physically* changed by changing our thinking. He contends that chemical and electromagnetic pathways enable energy, in the form of our beliefs, to affect our biology—in other words, our *thoughts* are so powerful that science has shown that they have the capacity to alter the structure of our DNA (*molecular change*).

In the next few chapters the idea of "mental riding"—using our thoughts, our beliefs, our mind—from my previous book, *Dressage for the New Age*, will be further elucidated. I consider my life's work to be expressing the importance of the mental element in combining human and horse, and now we will examine it through a scientific lens in terms of its role in

Molecular Equitation. At long last, the scientific community has provided information that explains just how essential our thoughts and emotions are in our riding and our connection to our horses.

a molecular summary

The previous pages lay out the key elements that we will explore in the following chapters. New discoveries in quantum physics have revolutionized our understanding of the experience of *connection* (via communication) and *consciousness*. The "molecular formula" is simple and can be summarized as follows:

Communication is facilitated between living beings by:

1

*Molecules as the vehicles of
information transfer.*

2

*The existence of a quantum
"web of connection" or "field" where
information transfer is faster than we
ever thought possible.*

3

*Our DNA acting as a transducer, leaving
an imprint of our information on
everything we touch.*

4

*Emotions as the elixir to maintain
and enhance that communication.*

Harnessing the power of human emotion is the catalyst—the key ingredient in this formula. Our ability to create a *feeling* and stay in it is key. Drawing on quantum physics research, we are reminded by author Gregg

Braden that there are three key three elements that set the quantum "field" apart from any other energy of its kind:

1

This field exists all around us.

2

Experiments suggest that it has its own "intelligence."

3

This field of energy responds to the emotions of living beings.

These elements, along with the "molecular formula" provided on p. 15, have the potential to maximize our experience with our horses in a way previously never thought possible by many equestrians. These are the ingredients that great horsemen feel, great communicators know, and great healers give.

a new paradigm

I want to introduce a *new paradigm* that elevates the existing hierarchical outline of "lightness" that has been presented within the horse industry until now. When I use the term "lightness," I mean being with the horse as he is truly collected, on the bit, with maximum impulsion and a slack rein, with brilliance, beauty, and *life*.

This new paradigm will serve as the "lay of the land" and a template for much of what is discussed in the following chapters. It includes the "molecular parallels" to my existing mantra of riding art, creating a new "Molecular Mantra": The new parallels to *Direction, Rhythm, Bend,* and *Lightness* are *Concentration, Energy, Physicality,* and *Openness/Release.*

These parallels serve as the building blocks that comprise the "bubble" of "molecular lightness." Their sequential order results in the *Openness and Release* that characterizes lightness, oneness, and enlightenment.

Direction	Concentration
Rhythm	Energy
Bend	Physicality
Lightness	Openness/Release

Direction involves being able to *concentrate on one thing*. That may be focusing on where you are going with the horse. It can be directing your attention to an object or to a thought. *Direction* requires self-discipline, and it is the first thing that you must achieve in riding.

The next is *Rhythm*. When you find and keep a distinct rhythm, you find and keep the same balance, *the same energy that the rhythm dictates*. For example, when you are dancing with a partner to salsa music, you get a great feeling of happiness and carry yourselves in a balance and with an energy that relates to that happiness. With a slow dance, or music in a minor key, you will feel "blue" and perhaps sadness, and the energy you emanate will reflect that.

Bend is the *physical position* that ensures the horse's well-being and allows mental communication between rider and horse once the horse is on the bit. Mental communication is facilitated when there is no resistance, no force, no blocking, no aggression. The horse is relaxed and open to mirror the relaxed and open rider.

Lightness is *condicio sine qua non* (without it, there is nothing). It is the result of the horse being "on the bit" and the classical French riding goal *descente de main et de jambes*—the relaxing of the rider's hands and legs (a cessation of action...*release*). In addition, the key to understanding lightness is through recognition of the superior matter, the greater power that we are part of and that is inherent in us. This is the power we need to have when riding. The popular mantra used in some meditative practice in the journey to self-realization is *Om Namah Shivaya*—meaning you are *open to* and acknowledge (and indeed "bow to") your *true inner self*, which is *the form of God in you*.

This is our connection to something bigger than who we are, and it is what facilitates the creation of "oneness" with the horse. It is what creates the very thing that is so extraordinary—*molecular change*. It is through the circle created by the Molecular Mantra of *Direction*, *Rhythm*, *Bend*, and *Lightness*, and its parallel elements *Concentration*, *Energy*, *Physicality*, and *Openness/Release*, that we arrive at a molecular process—an *intermolecular exchange of energy* that leads to *molecular change* in human and horse. All these elements, in their order, need to be honored for union to occur.

small, simple tasks

The molecular process starts when *we are present* (being right here, right now, focused on this very moment) and when *we have defined goals*. We are mentally and physically available. In that regard, communication begins as a state of mind and body. If, instead, we are "scattered" and without focus, we risk losing the very essence of what we are looking for.

It is important that one learns *how to be* and not just *how to do*. We need to begin riding with a very simple task, one that is meant to initiate the relationship with the horse. It could be as simple as establishing a walk as we focus on knowing where we are going (*Direction*) or find a particular *Rhythm*.

We should not necessarily be focused on passage or piaffe, even when riding those movements is one of our goals. This is very tricky because we learn throughout our life that when we want to *produce something* we have to *do something*. The sequence of first focusing on pursuing small, simple tasks with our horse may seem, on the surface, as if nothing is happening; however, in the end when all the basic building elements come together, we have something incredible.

I learned this from my grandfather. He loved inventing things. He loved making his mind work. He was a locksmith by profession and knew everything about locks—he could pick every one. Consequently, his mind worked backward. When beginning a new project, he would not work on the "project" itself but on preparing for it: He would gather the necessary tools, the needed materials, and organize the different parts. He carefully measured and weighed everything. To us children, it seemed that for days he was doing nothing, which drove us crazy. However, when my grandfather did in fact start working on the project itself, the job was done quickly because of all the preparations made beforehand. This was a great lesson for me.

The sequence of first focusing on pursuing small, simple tasks with our horse may seem, on the surface, as if nothing is happening; however, in the end when all the basic building elements come together, we have something incredible.

When you approach a new lesson with your horse, do your "thinking" first. Use the power of your mind in the form of visualization (create a clear picture in your head of each movement, each interaction with your horse); work on your ability to be present; gather the basic building blocks of communication, which we just discussed. That way, when you are with your horse and beginning the communion that is riding, then everything is ready for your horse to meet you in the place where *molecular change* can occur.

There are many things you can do, without your horse, to prepare to be with him and prepare for the feeling you will experience when both of you come together. For example, you can, in the evening, sit in a quiet place and play a "movie" of your ride in your head. Do this with your eyes closed. This enables you to create a situation where you "mentally" ride your horse. Your movie can be as complete as you wish. It is a visual image of your state of being, your horse's, and the feeling that is the result of both of you *together*. For you, this movie is like being a pilot in a flight simulator.

misconceptions become barriers

Molecular change will occur when we want it to, when we have a clear *intention* (determination to act in a certain way). For most people, this may seem too simple a formula because it involves debunking previous notions of what training should be. But, because of the way I teach and train during my clinics, which are time-intensive, I am *unable* to be conventional. Years of working in this way have made me refine my ability to establish a quick rapport with a horse, assess his needs, and consider the next step in his training.

My work differs from regular training offered by others because the emphasis is not on the systematic training of the horse—and this might be a point of criticism by some. Because my time is limited, my priority becomes the *quality* of the relationship formed with the horse, and that facilitates his ability to learn. We can accelerate his learning—and even help "make things happen"—when we use our mind. It is because I am forced to adhere to a schedule that I rely on creating change in myself and the horse through mental clarity. This kind of approach is quite different from what is currently "out there"; it is a result of *the way I choose to be* as a teacher, as a clinician.

early lessons from mestre nuno oliveira

Very early one morning when I was in Portugal visiting the old *picadero* (riding school), Mestre Oliveira arrived riding an extremely large gray horse that was owned by a banker. He was a strange-looking horse: His back was slanted—I think he had once injured his haunches. Catching sight of me, Mestre asked me to ride the horse.

Wearing plain shoes and pants, I was not dressed properly, but still, I climbed into the saddle. The ring was very small, about 13.5 meters wide, maybe 27 meters long, room for a circle at each end. Mestre asked me to canter on a circle. He requested *descente de main et de jambes* (let go with the hands and the legs). Then he said, "Reins on the buckle." So I dropped the reins, and the horse stayed in the same position. Then he asked me to lengthen the stride down the long side, and in about five or six strides, I was at the other end. The gray was strong, and as I circled to the right, he was in a sort of galloping, big canter. Mestre asked me to collect the horse. Of course, I went to grab the reins, but he said, "Oh no...." And that was about the extent of it.

So then I stretched upward and pulled my shoulders back, and the whole horse came back in a collected canter—without any influence on the reins. Suddenly, this became one of the most important experiences of my life. I decided that *this* was what I wanted to learn and what I wanted to teach.

why lightness is considered the ultimate connection

Lightness—true collection on the part of the horse with maximum impulsion and a slack rein—*allows the horse to be himself*. Rein contact and strong leg contact, in many ways, interferes with the physical movement of the horse, and it totally destroys and alienates the horse's mind. Only when he is comfortable in the correct position, *and* light, do we have a chance to experience a superior understanding of the relationship between the two.

In fact, the horse is *already light* by nature. He experiences lightness under saddle only when he is ridden properly—in other words, it depends on how competent and tactful we are, how refined we are, in order for him to *just be himself*. When he is himself...he is light. When a horse has been "pulled on" for many years, a tactful rider is suddenly a new feeling. He must form a new understanding of being ridden—that he no longer has to answer to all the pushing of the rider's seat and legs, and pulling of the hands. The horse has to learn that this is not part of the equation anymore, and sometimes, this realization takes a certain amount of time. Once the horse does understand that the rider does not intend to interfere with his body or his mind, then it is only a matter of how clear the rider can continue to be...and *molecular change* will be able to happen at the discretion of the horse.

lightness is a perception of the rider

Lightness comes as a result of the rider's body and mind. First, the rider has to "get out of the way"—of what *is* (remember, the horse is already *light*). When the rider can do this and can put the horse in a correct position while maintaining enough energy to help the horse stay there, it is then that the dance will happen. The quality of the dance is dependent on the quality of the dancer, especially of he who leads.

A monk once said that *inviting God in is not enough*. You have to "get out" first—there is only space for one.

Getting out is the challenge.

The horse is already light by nature.

teachers as facilitators of
molecular change

While our horses are our best teachers, we cannot discount the importance of the simple human-to-human student-teacher relationship. There is much to be said about this as it allows for "learning" to go both ways. I think that a teacher can learn a lot from his student and vice-versa. The real "master" is the person who is able to show us the light, to direct us into a way that will allow *us* to understand what is happening, as he does.

There is a great responsibility on a teacher to direct his student in a certain way—a way that "awakens." When he imparts knowledge in an overwhelming way, too quickly, for example, instead of liberating the student, he "blocks" understanding. Therefore, the timing of teaching is very fundamental. When it is done well, the student will blossom. If knowledge is given too soon, the teacher could end up blocking his student's path to understanding with too much information before the student is ready to receive it.

The responsibility of the teacher is to feed the student what is needed at the time that it is needed—a principle of importance to the masters of the past. In this way, "learning" is not just a present-day interaction between student and teacher, but an important part of a long tradition of riders that have worked with a master in a certain way. I think that when people are really dedicated to such a tradition, it gives them a strong feeling of continuity; a strength of belonging.

learning is remembering

There is a Native American adage that says, "We do not learn, we remember." This means that at some point, we already "knew" all there is; in other words, our body, our mind, our soul already "knows" the subtleties of life and of riding. The only thing that we do is remember them through day-to-day experience.

We must think of being with our horse not as a matter of *learning* how to commune with him but a matter of *remembering* what our "higher self" already knows. Remembering more and more each time we ride becomes yet another opportunity for refinement.

the alchemy of lightness

old perceptions create room for new ones

To welcome in *the new*—new ideas, new potential—we need to consider the possibility that a different path to being with and riding a horse exists. Without judgment, with humility and compassion, we open ourselves to this possibility. We need to create change in ourselves in order to learn to look at things differently—let go of old perceptions and outdated knowledge. We need to be able to recognize that even *very little change* in the way we look at things can make a big difference. (I speak more to the importance of change later in the book—see p. 123.)

What follows are just some examples of misconceptions about horses that we hold to as being true. These are the very things that prevent us from creating a "different reality" with our horse—that of a vision nested in openness, a communion.

The following are just a few examples of common statements made about riding and horses that are *not* true:

Misconception 1
The horse is, for the most part, on the forehand.

Misconception 2
A young horse cannot be light.

Misconception 3
The horse's conformation is a barrier to lightness.

Misconception 4
Lightness is achieved as an end goal of training.

Misconception 5
*Lightness (in the horse) comes from a lot of hard work
(on the part of the rider), namely pulling and pushing.*

Any changes in our understanding or consciousness are a result of self-discipline and practice. Understanding lightness and how it is attained is no different. We must practice being with our horse as we might practice meditation: every day in the same position, the same mind, the same spirit.

Check-In

Use these prompts to review the ideas we've discussed so far:

1

*Name the basic molecular components that are
essential in the process of transmutation.*

2

*Revisit the new additions to the Molecular
Mantra of riding.*

3

Explain how these molecular elements lead to lightness.

4

*Explore the misconceptions that we bring to our
relationship with our horse.*

chapter 2

When Two Become One

can "mental riding" become spiritual?

We are going from what I call "physical riding," with a knowledge of biomechanics and how the horse moves his body, into a mental state where we know that we are in tune with his mind and that the two beings— rider and horse—have become one. Then we are communicating together.

"Physical riding" is a little bit like when people practice yoga and they look at the physical exercise, but they don't understand that yoga is also highly spiritual, and therefore, it catches them by surprise. A person may discover lots of different levels of physical and spiritual benefit, or not, depending on the richness of the person and what he or she is looking for. It is like walking in the river looking for gold: We will find gold if we think there is gold in there; if we don't think there is gold in there, we will not even look for it.

This other "spiritual" level is really another dimension, if I can say that— it is definitely the molecular level we are talking about, far away from the basic biomechanical and physical aspects of riding.

Our mind provides our intellect and our ability to learn—our ability to put academic things together. And then we have another side of our mental self that is spiritual in nature. It is the spiritual part of our mind—perhaps we can call this *the soul*—that allows us to experience different levels of consciousness. It is this spiritual part of our mental self that is integral to our work with horses.

Attaining different levels of consciousness is a progressive state: We begin as a basic, physical person. Then we become a little more mentally aware as we start to think and to truly understand the power of our mind. Eventually, we begin to understand something that is a lot bigger than our mind—*our soul*, the part of us that is our spirit, our supreme being, our highest self.

"We are all connected. We swim in a sea of light, which is the zero point field. [The illusion of] separateness is the biggest problem of the world."

Lynne McTaggert, Author of *The Field*

"togetherness" seen through a scientific lens

We have touched on the mental and spiritual aspects of finding "togetherness" with our horse, but what can science add to help explain how the process of "centaurization" (the union where horse and human become one) can occur?

the alchemy of lightness

To begin, recent research has invited us to view our world as a unified living organism: Contrary to the theories of Newton, Descartes, and Bacon, who believed that humans operate as machines with separate parts, we are actually all interconnected, and our own well-being is dependent on the well-being of the rest of nature. James Lovelock[32] is credited in the modern era with originating the concept of the earth as a single living system, and Fritjof Capra[33, 34] showed with undeniable and compelling logic how this can be: In his benchmark book, *The Turning Point*, he describes the universal relationships that bind all things, organic and inorganic, animate and inanimate, together into one indivisible whole.

Studies documenting the connection between human consciousness and other life forms, such as plants, have been conducted and replicated in an attempt to prove such universal relationships.[35] For example, Peter Tompkins and Christopher Bird, authors of *The Secret Life of Plants,* provide just one example that illustrates the fascinating account of the physical, emotional, and spiritual relations that operate between plants and humans.[36] In addition, Dr. Ken Hashimoto, Chief of Research and Development at Fuji Electronics Industries, has written for years about how nothing in the physical world operates without being affected, at a fundamental level, by consciousness. His book, *Introduction to ESP*, established the basis under which, for example, plants have become regularly used as truth detectors in the Japanese criminal court system. His second book, *Mysteries of the Fourth Dimensional World*, provides a comprehensive documentation of experimental results that have been replicated and that demonstrate the connection between the physical world and consciousness.[37]

Despite evidence of universal connection between beings, such as mentioned above, until recently, there had been relatively little research to help explain the actual "hows" and "whys" of the process of connection between horse and human, specifically. It is through some preliminary studies that we finally get a glimpse of how that process might occur.

For example, in one study conducted by Dr. Ellen Gehrke in collaboration with the Institute of HeartMath (a global leader in researching emotional physiology and the physiology of heart-brain research)[15], it was shown that there are indications that the horse responds to changes in human *emotional states*. Part of the study protocol included comparing heart rhythm (heart rate pattern) measurements of both a horse and his handler during prescribed emotional and procedural periods. (Note: Dr. Gehrke's work with what is known as *heart rate variability*, or *HRV*, is too complex to examine in depth here and I encourage further reading—see references on p. 133.) Interestingly, results suggested that a kind of synchronicity occurs between horse and human when they work together, and researchers concluded that horses are particularly sensitive to changes in human emotions. The study group suggests that this emotional communication may be mediated by an "energetic form of communication." In other words, it is likely that our own "internal landscape" influences an immediate change in the horse's physical action.

To further understand "togetherness" of horse and rider, we must begin to understand that the entire earth, operating as a single coherent system, behaves like an enormous electric circuit.[38, 39] Russian researchers[40] have linked electromagnetic radiation waves in the Extremely Low Frequency (ELF) range (frequencies from 3 to 300 Hz) to a variety of seemingly unrelated psychic phenomena, helping to explain our connection to other life forms. For example, thoughts produced by our brain can directly affect the ELF waves generated by another living being. They also discovered that the inverse is true—ELF waves can and do influence the inner workings of the human brain and can be used to induce specific emotional effects.[41] Much of the research about this phenomenon during the last 30 years has been conducted by the US Navy, to develop a variety of devices designed to harness ELF waves to support real-time communication with submarines. [42]

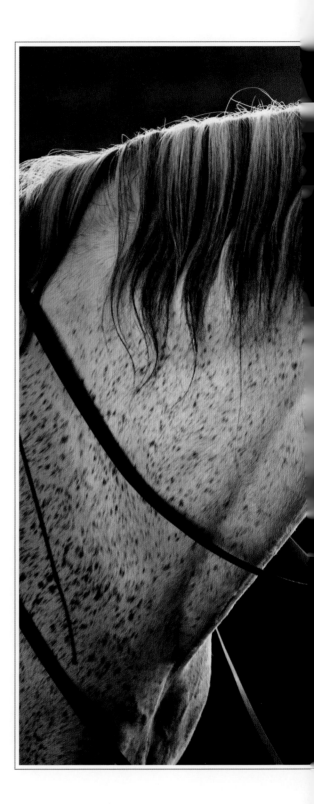

A kind of synchronicity occurs between horse and human when they work together.

Humans and horses, as mammals, are deeply and constantly affected by what is called the *Schumann resonances*—a set of spectrum peaks in the earth's ELF waves. These ELF waves have been shown to exert a measurable, demonstrable effect, which is individuated within humans and other species. Experiments and other investigations mentioned later in this book tell us that human emotions, behaviors, and health can be deeply affected by the transmission of finely tuned ELF waveforms. The fact that such effects are specific to both individuals and groups of humans, as well as other life forms, suggests that the architecture of living creatures on earth has evolved in a way that is inextricably interconnected with one of the fundamental energetic phenomena that characterize the planet itself.

Breathing has one of the strongest and clearest effects on our body, and offers the most direct way to influence beings around us.

Why are ELF waves important to understanding "togetherness" of horse and rider? The signals from our body affect life forms around us. Interestingly, a basic life function—breathing—has one of the strongest and clearest effects on our body, and offers the most direct way to influence beings around us. Hungarian philosopher of science Ervin László's studies show, for example, that the wave form associated with the *Schumann resonance* (a set of spectrum peaks in the earth's ELF waves) at 7.83 cycles per second is virtually identical to the brain-wave pattern exhibited by Tibetan monks and seasoned meditators who have achieved a deep meditative state via control of the breath.[43] Research on the effects of group meditation suggests that it is possible that individuals engaged in meditative breathing techniques can experience congruent brain waves, which in turn could mean that we can transmit information via an energy field, directly affecting the brain waves operating in other humans and animals nearby.[44]

In another study volunteers were taught to change their heart rate patterns by simply breathing slowly. They were instructed to collectively slow their breathing while focusing on another untrained group at a distance. What was found was just short of astonishing: Preliminary results indicated that when *intention* (determination of breath and heart rate pattern change) was directed *by* the trained group *toward* the untrained group, a statistically significant number of them *also* experienced a notable increase in their *heart rhythm coherence* (described by the Institute of HeartMath as "a highly efficient and regenerative functional mode associated with increased co-herence in heart rhythm patterns and greater harmony among physico-logical systems"). Researchers concluded that perhaps this is suggestive of an energy field that can be generated and enhanced by our *intention* (see p. 103 for further discussion of *intention*).[45]

the perfect relationship with the horse

Lightness starts with a relationship, with the belief that the horse has a desire to dance and a desire to share time and space with us. A perfect relationship is when we do not pre-judge nor do we assume we know the horse, and when we have no expectations. This is a state of "neutral think-ing," and when we go into neutral thinking, accepting the horse as he is, we will soon "see" the horse "coming to" us. Basically, we can then ask him if he wants to dance, and if he says yes, then we may begin.

A perfect relationship with the horse is when we do not pre-judge nor do we assume we know the horse, and when we have no expectations.

When we approach the horse expecting something from him, it puts us into a situation of "needs"—for the horse, this is too much, too over-whelming. (I explain how to let go of expectations in the pursuit of light-ness later on—see p. 75.)

It seems that the stronger our desire to change something, to "make it happen," the more elusive our power is to do so. This is because what we want is so often based on ego. As we mature into a state of consciousness where we *know* that we can alter our reality, however, it also seems that it becomes less important for us to do so. It is this freedom of possessing "power" without attaching so much importance to it that allows us to be even more effective in our prayers, requests, and desires. When we are able to "go into the bubble," as I call it, we are able to find and be in a space where everything is okay. It is there that we are able to have the relation-ship we desire with a horse—or with another human being.

In order to bring the horse into this "bubble," the space where everything is okay, we longe him and do work in hand. Putting him into a position where he can relax, where he can feel comfortable, allows him to feel some contentment, some happiness, some well-being. Then he, too, is in that space where intermolecular energy exchange is at its best.

For the "physical rider," communication is often at first: "Put the music on and do a series of dance steps." But after that, when the dance steps are done, the same rider can discover a whole different level of expressing him- or herself in the dance; a whole different level of "being one" with a partner; a whole different level, and in fact, a *sublimation* of the dance. I think the transmutation we touched upon earlier in this book comes when a rider is in that state, as it is then the rider can start to sense the energy exchange that can lead to *molecular change*.

Now, this being said, the rider may still ask, "Why do I have a hard time communicating with my horse and feeling what is going on between us?" Well, mostly it is because we are *too busy*. We are not in that "okay space" or "bubble" that I just described. We have all sorts of agendas and things to do, and we want to do as well as we did yesterday or better, and we want to do this, and we want to do that. We have all these *goals*, and all these *expectations* that block our mind. And we resort to physicality, to kicking, pulling, pushing with the seat—all kinds of mechanical, physical stuff that is in the way of being in that *good molecular space*. This leads us to wanting *even more* to communicate with the horse, so we do *even more* physically—more "stuff."

When we are in the physical space I just described, we are unable to really *feel* anything, because *instead of being, we are doing*. It is very important that we come to understand that we can *be* and not *do*. Once this is attained, it is just a matter of practicing to elevate our awareness, our understanding, to a higher level.

Staying in that consciousness of *just being, not doing*, maintaining that energy, is very difficult. When practicing meditation, for example, we have a series of techniques that help us in this area, mostly through the use of breath. Becoming aware of our breathing can help us arrive at a different level of consciousness and then stay there. With practice, this is fairly basic.

What is difficult—what is our *human challenge*—is to be able to function in the world while keeping that *mindfulness* or level of awareness. It is very challenging to sit on a horse, for example, and feel that we are *with him* and stay *with him* without any stoppage, any barriers, any break in awareness. It takes practice because we are all changing all the time. As we've shown in the pages before, any change in our emotions affects the horse, and any change in the horse affects us, eliciting other feelings, perhaps not so much within our control. To keep steadily *with* our horse, enveloped in the mental state of love and "oneness," is difficult. We must practice, practice, practice.

"It takes more than a regular state of consciousness to make a 'quantum possibility' a present reality. The great secret to bringing the focus of our imagination, beliefs, healing, and peace into a present reality is that we must do so without a strong attachment to the outcome."

Amit Goswami, Author of *The Quantum Doctor*

how emotions affect our relationship with the horse

There are two primary kinds of emotions that impact our relationship with the horse: fear and love. When we approach horses or other people with fear in our heart, they will respond in fear. If we approach them with love, then they are inclined to respond in kind. This has to do with the intermolecular energy exchange and the shared energy field we have already discussed.

Therefore, what we have to do is define the "love frequency"—the electromagnetic energy frequency emitted from our body that makes us comfortable with each other and with other living beings. In addition, this "love energy vibration" has been found to encourage healing and boost creativity. This is a much lower frequency than what we are used to—people who are nervous, for example, can experience difficulty in "moderating their frequency." Their nervousness can make their energy erratic. In general, people are scared, and we have all seen how fear works as a control mechanism. When we have a partner we dominate with fear, our relationship is ugly and malformed.

The only way forward is to transmute fear into true love—unconditional love—and then whatever is happening is just fine. This process is about

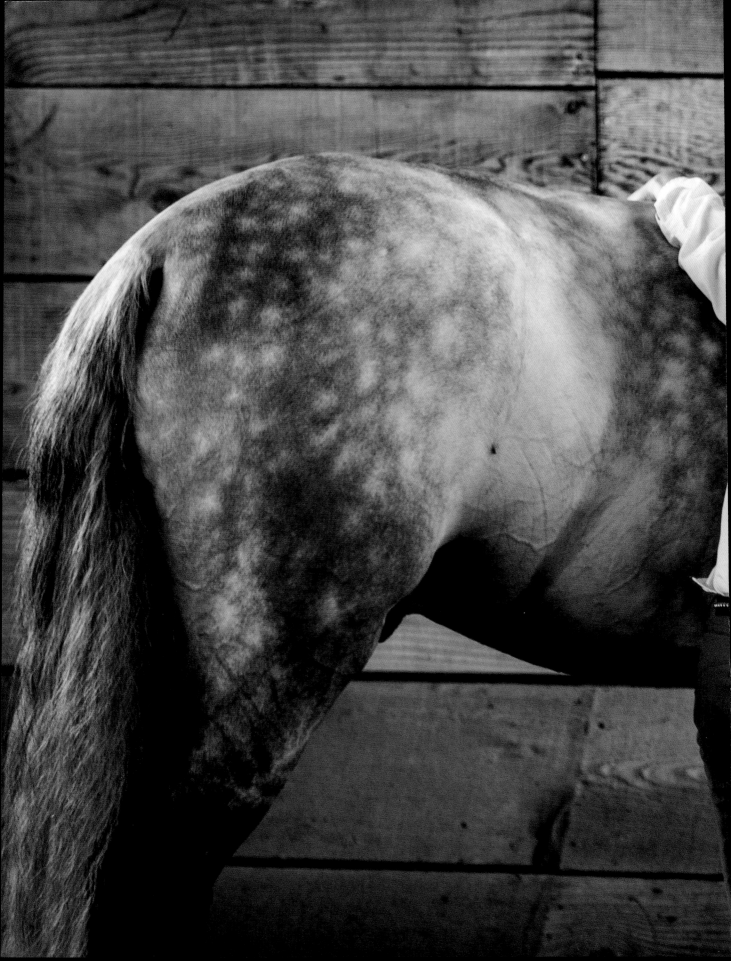

When we approach the horse with love in our heart, he will respond in kind.

accepting, for the present moment, what is. I think that only in a state of love, in a state of kindness, can we achieve that. We have to reach deep down where the electromagnetic frequency between us and the world is welcoming and absorbing, and only then are we tapping into a channel of communication on a different level (see my discussion of ELF beginning on p. 30).

Cultivating the feeling of love allows us to tap into the "love frequency." It is the exact opposite of fear, anger, or hate. Love and compassion are skills in which we can train ourselves. As mentioned already, researchers have identified frequencies[48-56] achieved by slow breathing and commonly associated with meditative practices that elicit feelings of wellness and calm (p. 32). In addition, in a pilot study at the University of California, San Francisco, researchers found that schoolteachers briefly trained in Buddhist techniques and who meditated less than 30 minutes a day experienced improvements in their mood, to the same degree as would be expected if they had taken antidepressants.[57, 58]

The proof is in the pudding!

love and the principles of lightness

The following are the basic principles that facilitate molecular "togetherness" and lightness:

Principle 1

*The horse must be in the correct position—
on the bit.*

Principle 2

*This position, as it is achieved and then
maintained, must be comfortable for the horse,
leading to true relaxation and promoting
overall well-being.*

Principle 3

*We must understand different kinds of energy
and how they affect us and the horse.*

In our pursuit of lightness, we do not need the kind of energy often relied on: nervousness created by fear, fear created by spurs, movement forced and taken from the horse. We need positive, calm, light, loving energy. Relaxed movement will then be willingly given by the horse.

This positive energy is where beauty comes from in equestrian art. More importantly, this energy opens the door to a different world; a never-ending communication with our horse. The limits, here, are our own. In this space everything is one mind-body-spirit. Very few problems occur between human and horse, perhaps even none at all. With the feeling of oneness comes the sensitivity that allows us to "pre-feel" as we are riding—that is, to sense those tiny imperfections in movement and communication that can become major concerns in a very short time. This "pre-feeling"—a positive kind of anticipation—becomes a wonderful aid in our journey toward lightness; being mindful of future imperfections will help us prevent them from intruding in our dance.

can we transcend fear molecularly?

To rise above the energy of fear, first we have to examine the very basis of what fear is and determine what we are going to do with it.

Generally, we fear what we do not know. For example, people are often afraid of horses—and other animals—because they do not know enough about them. They may not have sufficient knowledge or understanding to be safe around horses. For example, something as simple as not being aware of what may happen if we unexpectedly walk up behind a horse can cause a reaction in the horse that reinforces our fear. With study and with experience, we learn that we need to say, "Hello," by approaching the horse within his line of sight and that there is a code of "etiquette" so the horse recognizes that we are a friend, not a predator.

Therefore, when a student is afraid of horses, I advise him or her to take a book and a chair and go inside the horse's paddock or stall and *just sit there*. After a while the horse will come and nuzzle the student, and he or she will do what comes naturally and say, "Hey, how are you? Are you doing okay?" And the horse will do his little nibbling and the person will do a little talking and soon the person will get used to the way the horse moves and breathes and reacts. After a while, the student will say, "I am okay with this—it is no big deal."

Another reason people are afraid of horses is that they are afraid of falling off them. When someone gets on top of a horse, consciously or unconsciously, any feelings of being "grounded" or secure are taken away. The rider must trust the horse enough to make him a keystone—the foundation of the rider's physical self.

But before trust such as this is possible, we have to go through a lot, a *lot* of self-examination because fear is generally ruled by our ego. Our ego tells us, "No, no, no…don't do this. This is not good for you." The ego is actually there to protect us, to take care of us, and the way it does that is, "No, no, no…you cannot…you are afraid." Learning more about horses, about how to interact with them and trust them—and have them trust us—is one step to overcoming the ego's overprotectiveness. In addition, understanding that we are the creators of our own world and that we can decide to live each day in the "love frequency" (see p. 38) will facilitate positive change in all areas of our life and being—another step toward transcending the ego.

Remember, there are only two kinds of emotions important to finding lightness on the back of a horse: love and fear. What is wonderful about these emotions is that if energy is not derived from one, then it is from the other. Therefore, when asked the question, "Can we transcend fear molecularly?" the answer is, "Yes, by replacing it with love."

By replacing the molecular energy of fear with the molecular energy of love:

1

We are no longer afraid.

2

We are comfortable.

3

When we are comfortable, we can be closer (in body and mind) to the horse. And this is the time when the molecular change happens. It is about being able to "be one"—to be comfortable—with ourselves first. Then we can take our pick on what or who we want to be one with—the ocean, the mountains, with an animal, or another person.

When becoming one with another being, we need the animal or person to be just as comfortable as we are, to arrive in a "comfort zone" where everyone is okay with everyone else. *Then* we have the possibility of the *molecular change* that creates the "togetherness" everyone is looking for—unconditional love. When one part of the equation is an animal or person who is afraid or anxious or experiencing physical discomfort, then the energetic exchange can be everything else—but it is not lightness, and it is not a relationship.

When we are able to "be one"—to be comfortable—with ourselves first, we can then take our pick on what or who we want to be one with.

finding "grounding" and creating trust

Unconsciously, and most of the time, riders do not realize that when they get on the back of a horse, they lose their natural means of "grounding," by which I mean the connection of the energy coming from the earth and to their "human energy field" (and their body), primarily through their feet. When we ride, grounding occurs via the four legs of the horse, which means the rider becomes dependent on what the horse is doing, or going to do, for centeredness and balance. This is a drastic change from our normal two-legged existence, and we must learn to trust in the horse as we trust in ourselves.

The role of the teacher in this changeover is of importance: He must longe the rider to help the rider realize the change in grounding; to encourage enjoyment of the process; and to create an energy that allows the rider—and the horse—to relax. When the relaxation comes, both rider and horse understand that they are safe, and when they are safe they start to enjoy it, and when they start to enjoy it they start to love it, and when they start to love it...it is done.

the horse as a conduit of enlightenment

As we have discussed, it is a different state of consciousness that allows both the rider and the horse to *be* and *stay* one. This union, mind-body-spirit, can be the closest thing to the expression of "God" that man can experience in this human life. The horse becomes a conduit of enlightenment. He allows us to become much bigger in spirit, consciously connected to all.

I have been teaching others how to work with horses for about 40 years. I see the same situation all the time. There are people who do not understand and who do not *want* to understand these concepts because their instinct is to attack first. I would say about 50 percent of people have a problem with the ideas I'm exploring in this book because they think they cannot achieve lightness with compassion. Because they cannot conceive how it is possible, they fight it. The result is many people in essence *fight the lightness* because they cannot "get it," because they are pulling all the time. The kind of contact they rely on in the saddle is *not* the contact that I refer to—it is pulling. They are pulling because they are scared—and that brings us right back to ego, and to the emotions of love and fear (see p. 39).

Not too many people want to hear this; however, it is the truth.

visualization to facilitate communication

Visualization is a powerful mental tool in working with horses. I wrote in *Dressage for the New Age* that it is like we are watching television with our horse—our goal is to bombard the screen with images of how we envision a movement, a moment, a perfect microsecond. We must *visualize what we want*. Note that this is on a personal level and actually has nothing to do with the horse. In other words, the architect can envision a house already built on a specific piece of land before he sits at the drafting table. The interior decorator, in an empty room, is able to see in his head how the space should be used, a palette, furniture, accessories. The businessman can imagine an entire marketing and growth plan for, and potential earnings of, a successful enterprise.

Visualization is what we see. I feel that *see* is a very important word because *when we see, we actually create.* When I look at a horse and *see* the end result—what that horse can potentially be—then that *visualization* tells me how to achieve this result. It provides a "blueprint" to follow. Therefore, the first thing riders must do, through self-discipline, is train themselves to *see* a better blueprint: a detailed blueprint *in color* (if I can say that); a blueprint with feelings, with music, utterly complete in their mind. This is the creative process of an artist.

Feeling is a language: how to create the feel, how to project the feel, how to keep the feel. Visualization is a blueprint with feeling. *How* do we want to feel? *What* do we want to feel? We can tap into our memory bank of past feeling and use what we've felt other times to actualize new feeling *before* it is experienced. To visualize with feel, we must close our eyes, and *ride* it. It is a simple thing, really.

We must also have established a means of communication with the horse that physically, mentally, and molecularly allows him to understand what we are *seeing* and what we are *feeling*. I believe that animals communicate with pictures; that this idea of visualization is not extraordinary for horses, since I think it is how they "talk." As soon as they receive an image from us, as soon as they know what we want and what we are looking for, they will try to mimic as carefully as possible what they see on our shared television screen. Therefore, the clarity of the picture is fundamental.

After a while, horses are able to "send" us pictures, in return. For me, this is the most interesting part of our evolving communication—receiving "images" from the animals. It happens all the time, I think, and the more sensitive we are, the more we know it is possible and that it is happening constantly. We need to be in the "bubble" I mentioned on p. 33 and be in "molecular harmony"—the intermolecular energy exchange in progress— in order to feel reciprocated visualization from the horse. I always say, "It is *not* important for a monkey to learn 100 words of human language; it is *very* important for humans to learn 100 words of monkey language." In other words, it is more important for the human to understand the animal—what he has to say, his way of communicating it, what he feels, and then, allowing him to express it.

riding what we think is possible

I had an absolutely great day with a friend's horse: I was able to request and get the passage with just *the feel* and the *intent of the feel* so that the horse, Herodes, was able to enjoy the movement, take it, and do nothing else—there was no interference of any kind on my part (physical or mental). I wanted to keep the passage and turn it toward the center of the arena, but Herodes felt, in his mind, that he needed the wall, that it was helping him. Therefore, I did it on both sides of the ring, right and left, and only then did I ask for it in the center. And he was absolutely extraordinary! His tendency was to be on his left shoulder and put his nose to the right; I asked him to do the reverse, putting his nose to the left and getting off that left shoulder, and he did it, instantly, like a refined person would do—and sort of with a "smile."

You see, horses are able to understand so much more than we think they can. Their understanding is limited only by what *we* think is possible—or not possible—with them...what *we* think their limitations are. We can open the floodgates of understanding when *we* strive to understand them first.

The horse's understanding is limited only by what we think is possible.

the alchemy of lightness

Let me share another story. I had a Portuguese dog named Spot, and he came with me to the United States. People would ask the name of my dog, and I'd say, "Spot," and it was really quite funny that this little Portuguese dog's name was one of the most common dog names in America!

He was a little terrier, a little "street kid," and he was part of a gang of about 20 dogs. Every morning we would wake up together, and we would sing a happy (doggy) song, "Woof, wooooof, wooof!!!" Then we had a rainy-day song that sounded like a doggy growl: "Grrrrr, aougrrrrrr." Then we had sort of an in-between song, kind of a mixture of both, that meant just, "I don't want to get up." So every morning we had either a happy song, a sad song, or an in-between song.

Then one day it was a very sunny day, and I was feeling great when we woke up, "It's a really sunny day, it's great! Woof, wooooof, wooof!!!" and he turned to me and said, "Grrrrrr." I was taken aback because it was a beautiful day! So far he had always mimicked me in our little game, but on that day, he was like, "For me, it's *not* a good day, so shut up!"

Animals are always talking to us. With horses it's the same. Not only do they have pictures but they have a lot of things to tell us in different ways. Recently I was working with a horse, and he clearly told me not to push it. He told me, "Do what you have to do, but nothing new and nothing different, please." That communication, that understanding, was great. The same horse the day before had allowed me to try new things, but on that day he asked me to just be nice, be calm, be quiet, be compassionate.

And I listened, and rode what I thought possible.

visualization seen through a scientific lens

What is the process that happens when we use our imagination, focus, and *visualize* what we want to create with our horse? How can science explain what happens? We get a glimpse of how this occurs through several experiments conducted by the Institute of HeartMath (see p. 29). The experiments suggest that what we consider the creative process is in actuality *already occurring*. What we *think* we experience spontaneously in effect already exists. Put simply, the Institute of HeartMath's experiments give credence to the practice of visually imagining and rehearsing our dream ride.

In one experiment, study participants stared at a blank white computer screen. After a period of a few seconds, an image came up on the monitor.

One set of images was designed to calm the participants, as measured by brain and heart rhythm responses, and the other set of images was designed to produce emotional arousal. The images were generated at random by the computer according to the International Affective Picture System (IAPS)—a set of images that have been standardized for use in research to elicit a range of emotions and are thought to be universal in effect.

The truly astonishing finding of this experiment was that participants' heart *and* brain responded *before* the random image generator in the computer had generated any image at all and several moments *before* the computer presented it to the subject,[58, 59] suggesting that *emotion* may be the catalyst for precognition (clairvoyance related to an event or state not yet experienced).[60] In other words, participants were not spontaneously reacting to images generated by the computer. Their emotional response began before they actually viewed an image.

So, to imagine our dream ride is to understand and believe that everything we do *out of the saddle* prepares us for optimal communion with the horse *in the saddle*. We can get excited and feel the joy in our ride *before* we are there, and it is this emotional response, felt prior to our ride, that can result in a reality to match.

how to assess oneness

When we find ourselves wondering what the status is—that is, whether we have attained *oneness* with our horse—well, that means we haven't. When we are *one* with nature; when we are *one* with music; when we are *one* with somebody, we are just simply *one*, and not busy assessing it. The very word "assessing" refers to a totally intellectual state, and oneness has *nothing* to do with intellectual thinking. We cannot mix a word from one system (logical, intellectual) with another (pure feeling, emotional). And as mentioned earlier in this book, the "mental" self we are most interested in for achieving lightness is spiritual, not intellectual. When we experience oneness we are in a different state of consciousness: We know when we are there and when we are not. It is a black-and-white experience.

When we go through the learning process with the horse—that is, creating our partnership with him, learning to dance with him, and to communicate with him both in and out of the saddle—we have to learn the basics. It is like when we learn to play the piano, and we are first taught where to place our fingers. Once we get the basic mechanics of moving our fingers, it becomes automatic—we do not even have to think about it anymore. When we still have to think about the mechanics of doing something, then we have not yet integrated the basics.

Riding a horse is the same. We have to learn the basics first until gradually, our physicality is automated and we are "doing" less and less. *Then* we can arrive at a certain spot where we start to *feel*.

Consciousness is not something we can measure or test. I am sure there is some way that some claim they can say that a certain person is at a given level (of consciousness), since our tendency is to measure everything, but the general understanding is that when we attain oneness, we simply *feel* that we are there. The more we feel it, the more we are there, the more we are able to *stay* there, maintaining that feeling. Practice, practice, practice.

creating oneness seen through a scientific lens

Researchers from the Institute of HeartMath[13] have compiled evidence to suggest that there is an "electrical force," an energy field that allows us to *feel* and *be with* another being, even at great distances. Theirs is the first research group to successfully attempt to directly measure an energy exchange between people and provide a testable theory to explain the feelings of connectedness that we experience with each other and with other beings. They suggest that it is *the heart* that provides a method of bioelectromagnetic communication within and between beings. It is the heart that produces the largest electromagnetic field in the body, and earlier studies suggest that the heart's energy has the capacity to permeate cells and act as a synchronizing signal, carrying information in a way similar to radio waves.[61]

Researchers were able to show that when two individuals touch or are simply in proximity, one person's electrocardiogram (ECG) signal is registered in the other person's brain wave recordings. While the signal transmission was strongest when people were in contact, the effect was still detectable when participants were close but not touching. They conclude that this suggests that there exists a presence "of an unknown form of energetic or informational interaction" between beings. Consider what it means if we extend these findings to our relationship with horses.[62-65] The energetic frequency emitted by our heart can affect our horse, and vice versa, not only when we ride, but when we are simply near each other. Our systems are communicating, perhaps even before we have made a movement or spoken a word. It is here that oneness is within reach.

the role of the teacher

The most important thing for a *real* teacher in the realm of equestrian art is to facilitate *molecular change*. In the beginning, the student may have an intellectual idea about what he or she is trying to attain. However, as noted in our discussion of oneness, *molecular change* has nothing to do with the intellect, and a lot to do with something very physical and something very spiritual. *Molecular change* is not about reading a study in a book or journal and saying, "Okay, I understand that." It is about opening ourselves energetically and emotionally to allow that higher understanding to become part of our being. When the teacher creates the right kind of energy (think of that shared energy "field"), he enables the student and the horse to find a position where they start to engage in their own intermolecular energy exchange. Then the rider feels something different in himself, in his horse—he suddenly feels that *connection*. That is the beginning of oneness.

It is also the teacher who helps nurture an attitude in the horse that allows the change to happen. Then, he may have to calm his student, or encourage the student to find a different level of awareness, or find creative ways to help the student attain a different level of consciousness. Suddenly, with the right kind of energy managed by the teacher, the rider will *feel* what is going on between him or her and the horse—and this is, of course, the process of *molecular change*.

The master (teacher) looks at a rider and knows just how to guide him or her in order to allow these things to happen—a little bit like Merlin the wizard, the teacher can "touch it" and "the magic" happens. Once the rider feels *molecular change* as it is going on, there is a better chance of learning how to recreate it in the future.

The riding teacher and the student are similar to the guru and the seeker who goes for *Darshan* (the Hindu term that describes an interaction in presence between a devotee and a god, usually the receipt of blessings). Oftentimes, just the simple sight of the guru or a moment in his presence is enough to cause change within us. The word *guru* translates basically to mean "the person who dissipates the darkness." What does this mean? You *see the light* because the guru is able to *take the darkness out of you*.

*The teacher opens doors so that the student may see what is on the other side.
The student then decides whether to go through the door or not.*

When I talk about energy, visualization, and *molecular change*, I'm talking about the teacher being able to "hold" the horse and the rider in a certain energy that both allows them to *function* and enables them to *feel*. This is a complicated mixture. It is like making a cake. We have to put the right ingredients in, and then, if we don't burn it, it will be both beautiful and delicious; the wrong ingredients or handling, however, and the cake won't rise or won't taste good. Like the ingredients in the cake, the student, the horse, and the master mix together, but in a way that either allows or does not allow *molecular change* to happen.

teaching and learning across distance seen through a scientific lens

Researchers at the Institute of HeartMath[13] and the Institute of Noetic Sciences[66] have demonstrated the possibility of influencing someone from a distance. Russian researchers interested in understanding psychic phenomenon showed, through their study of ELF waveforms (see p. 30), that the possibility *does exist* to influence human behavior at a distance, by remote means.[40, 41] In a series of experiments using biofeedback measures (such as body temperature, for example), they were able to document the effects of mental influence of others.[12] In each session, participants were divided into "mental influencers," and those who would be the remote targets of the "influence." Influencers were instructed to either calm or activate a remote person's skin temperature activity. Influencers were successfully able to decrease and increase the skin temperature activity at a level that was statistically significant, thereby proving that humans can create change in other beings, even from a distance! It is with this evidence in mind that we must consider the true importance of the teacher's role in the development of horse and rider. It is the teacher's responsibility to provide the kind of mental "influence" that enables horse and rider to progress in a positive manner. These study results also support the idea that we can "influence" our horse, not only from his back, but from the end of a longe line, for example, or even without touching him at all.

Furthermore, in his book, *The Whispering Pond*,[43] Ervin László describes an experiment, conducted by a group of Italian scientists, in which the brain waves of individual meditators were evaluated first independently, and then together with the brain waves of other meditators who were physically close by but completely separated from the first group, as well as each other. By collecting measurements on brain-wave activity, researchers discovered that when two or more subjects meditate simultaneously, a *synchronization effect* is produced (ongoing behavior synchronizes with an ongoing stimulus).[43] If those who meditate can experience a *synchronization effect*, then it is perhaps not without possibility that teacher, rider, and horse can, as well—even when they are physically separated. This idea introduces the responsibility of the teacher, and of the rider, to create the right energy, to attain a state of consciousness, to control the breath and thus the heart-rate and brain-wave patterns that can meet the horse in the "present" where lightness awaits.

french classical principles facilitate molecular connection

Being open to considering that a molecular connection with our horse might be possible has much to do with the basic way that each of us looks at life. This includes what we are *willing to give* and what we are *ready to receive* in life. These two themes hold true in our work with horses. It is not *what we do* in the saddle, it is *who we are*.

Finding "togetherness" with the horse has nothing to do with nationality—there are, for example, some very "heavy" French riders, and there are some very "light" Germans. It has to do with the way we look at life. How much love can we put out there and thus minimize the level of discomfort we experience from day to day?

I mentioned oneness is about being able to give and to receive love. We must consider the proportion between what we can give and receive. Therefore, the "French" part of what now many call "French Classical Dressage" is a certain view of perfect balance and proportion—the perfection, balance, and proportion of the relationship between a horse and a man. The French classical style of riding is, therefore, where the oneness we want to have with our horse begins. That oneness only comes when we have a 50-50 partnership, one where the rider gets out of the way of the horse—physically and mentally—and does not feel that riding means constantly telling the horse what to do. Really, when we ride a horse, *he* is the one doing the work: We just sit there while he dances. We try to be *part of the dance* by being *part of the horse*. Practice allows us to feel that we are not moving separately but together—the beginning of "centaurization" (oneness).

French Classical Dressage is a visual representation of what we want to attain. And that vision, at a certain level, is what we dream of...what we desire. It is here the artistic element comes in as we "create" the ideal in our mind: How would we like our dream ride to happen? What would our dream ride be like?

Check-In

Use these prompts to review the ideas we've discussed so far:

1

What are the key molecular ingredients that enhance a sense of "togetherness"?

2

How does our emotional state affect our horse?

3

Explain the "heart connection" we can have with our horse.

4

How does energy affect the intermolecular energy exchange?

5

Explore the sense of becoming "one" with another being. How do we know when we have achieved "oneness"?

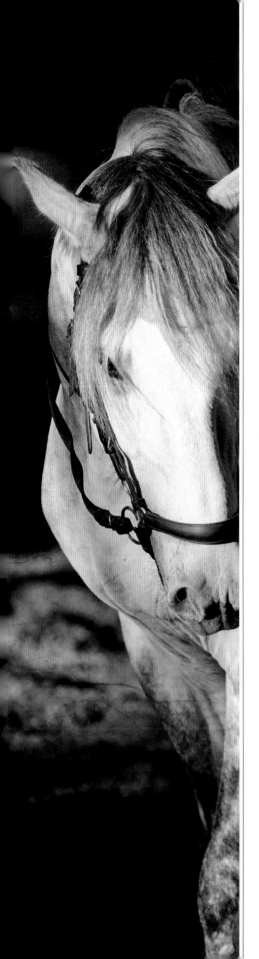

chapter 3

The Horse:
Healer, Teacher, Partner

the "mental contract" that needs to exist between horse and rider

I discussed the idea of a "mental contract" between horse and rider in my previous books *Dressage for the New Age* and *Meditation for Two*. A mental contract can be entered into after we have found a place of physical comfort for the horse. Then we can ask the horse, "Do you want to dance with me?" The horse considers whether or not to say, "Yes," and when he does, that is the original contract: We make sure the horse feels good, and in return, he agrees to dance with us.

But negotiations do not stop there. We have to play with the horse all the time...our work with him has to be fun, a relationship with two happy participants. The invitation to enter a mental contract becomes, "Do you want to play with me?" As a trainer or a rider we have to always think about the *joy* in riding because this feeling is not natural to a lot of people. Many riders take it too seriously. *Joy* and *play* are always there when working with horses...if we want them. We just need to get on the same level as our horse and say, "Hey, I want to play now, and then I want to dance, and if we dance we need to do this and that and that..." so the mental contract is saying "let's play together." Whether longeing, or schooling in hand, or riding, it can all be a dance and a lot of fun. But, when any of these things *becomes a bore*, then it becomes a *bad* dance.

Joy and play are always there when working with horses... if we want them.

healing *from* the horse and healing *of* the horse seen through a scientific lens

Recent studies conducted by the Institute of HeartMath[13] provide a clue to explain the bidirectional "healing" that happens when we are near horses. According to researchers, the heart has a *larger electromagnetic field* and *higher level of intelligence* than the brain: A magnetometer can measure the heart's energy field radiating up to 8 to 10 feet around the human body. While this is certainly significant, it is perhaps more impressive that the electromagnetic field projected by the horse's heart is five times larger than the human one (imagine a sphere-shaped field that completely surrounds you). The horse's electromagnetic field is also stronger than ours and can actually directly influence our own heart rhythm!

Horses are also likely to have what science has identified as a "coherent" heart rhythm (heart rate pattern), which explains why we may "feel better" when we are around them. Earlier I mentioned Dr. Ellen Gehrke's work with heart rate variability (HRV)[15]: Her work along with studies at the Institute of HeartMath have found that a coherent heart pattern or HRV is a robust measure of well-being and consistent with emotional states of calm and joy—that is, we exhibit such patterns when we feel positive emotions.

A coherent heart pattern is indicative of a system that can recover and adjust to stressful situations very efficiently. This is generally consistent with a prey animal whose very survival depends on being mindfully alert of danger, quick to react, but also quick to recover and resume normal activities. Oftentimes, we only need to be in a horse's presence to feel a sense of wellness and peace. In fact, research shows that people experience many physiological benefits while interacting with horses, including lowered blood pressure and heart rate; increased levels of beta-endorphins (neurotransmitters that serve as pain suppressors); decreased stress levels; reduced feelings of anger, hostility, tension, and anxiety; improved social functioning; and increased feelings of empowerment, trust, patience, and self-efficacy.

It is the heart that holds the horse's inner secrets and provides evidence to suggest that horses, just like us, emote and feel. And like ours, their inner state appears to be measureable. Any electrocardiogram (ECG or EKG) measures the electromagnetic signal that the heart uses to send information to the brain and the rest of the body on different levels. This electromagnetic energy tells the story about what is going on inside us, physically and emotionally. In a preliminary study conducted by Dr. Gehrke in collaboration with the Institute of HeartMath, ambulatory ECG recorders were placed on four horses to measure HRV during a series of different conditions and interactions, and evidence was found that suggests a horse's inner state is reflected in his heart rhythm (heart rate pattern), similar to humans and other mammals.[15]

This rather naturally leads us to the question of our horse's emotions—many people doubt the existence of "emotion" such as we experience it in the horse, but recent studies have perhaps begun to prove otherwise. For example, ethologists Dr. Marc Bekoff (*The Animal Manifesto: Six Reasons for Expanding Our Compassion Footprint*) and Dr. Jonathon Balcombe (*Second Nature: The Inner Lives of Animals*) have been exploring the emotions of animals. Their works summarize research suggesting that animals have an emotional and moral code that includes the capacity for pleasure.[67]

what do we wish for the horse?

Our wish for the horse is to provide him with the gift of training that maximizes his level of comfort and allows him to be able to perform a dance together with his rider. Therefore, first we must invite him into a position

We must invite the horse
into a position where he
is able to dance.

the alchemy of lightness

where he is *able to dance*. Then the goal is to have the horse so mentally and physically in harmony with us that *the dancing becomes what he wants to do*. It is in this balance that a transmutation—a change of consciousness—occurs, giving us that incredible feeling of oneness.

And what are the elements that contribute to the horse's comfort and thus make all this possible? Imagine that you are a horse. What would you need to be willing to dance with a human partner; to be fully aware of what is asked of you? The Molecular Mantra I described in *Dressage for the New Age* and at the beginning of this book (see p. 16 for more about it) illustrates the basic elements necessary for the dance, and here I have rephrased the last element to highlight that which ensures the horse's comfort:

1 Direction

We have to clearly visualize the direction in which we are traveling, as the horse needs to know where he is going.

2 Rhythm

This element is the balance and energy apparent in the horse's movement.

3 Bend

Knowledge of the biomechanics of the horse has helped to explain that establishing a light longitudinal bend through his body puts him in the best position to relax in his movement. This is, in effect, his physical centering.

4 On the Bit and Light

Being on the bit is both a mental and physical attitude that allows the horse to be 100 percent with his rider. Lightness, as we discussed earlier in the book, is the release, the cessation of action on the rider's part, the result of which gives all the beauty to the performance.

why direction is so important

When we are driving on a slippery road, it can happen that we turn the steering wheel to the right but the car goes to the left, out of our control. What do we do? Hopefully, we stop! But it is necessary to be able to communicate direction to our vehicle in order to get where we need to go safely.

When we are riding, direction is important for the same reason, but also because it illustrates the kind and quality of relationship we have with our horse. We should be clear about where the horse should place each footfall because the horse needs to have our clarity of purpose and direction. If instead we ride like our horse is a car on a slippery road, we try to overcorrect and face common pitfalls, namely that anything that *can* go wrong, *will* go wrong, because we do not have the necessary relationship with the horse. There is no connection. That means we are unbalanced, we start pulling, our horse starts fighting, our horse is rigid, our horse is crooked, and our horse takes off. When we try to dance with someone with whom we have no connection, it is very difficult and certainly neither beautiful nor flowing.

why i say "on the bit and light"

Here, I rephrased the last element in the Molecular Mantra from simply *Lightness* to *On the Bit and Light*, because the "on the bit" position is absolutely necessary to the willingness of the horse and our ultimate ascension to oneness. Visualization of *Direction*, *Rhythm*, and *Bend* facilitate bringing the horse on the bit. I am often amazed when I see pictures of renowned equestrians riding *without* the horse on the bit. It does not *look* nor does it *feel* correct. When we recognize that an intermolecular energy exchange with your horse is a possibility, then we also see that it is only in this position (on the bit) that the horse is happily able to do what is asked. As a rider and as a trainer it is fundamental.

On the other side of the coin, when the horse is "above the bit," he is fighting you and your aids and cannot form that mental contract with you (see p. 53). When he is too low and deep, in a rollkur or hyperflexed position such as described by Dr. Gerd Heuschmann[69] in his books and symposiums, the resulting movement and way of moving has been proven to be absolutely harmful to the horse, both mentally and physically. Biomechanics studies have proven that *the horse hurts* in such a position.

Above the bit or hyperflexed positions cannot and do not lead to oneness. The only position that works when true lightness is our aim, and the only position (most) everyone understands to be correct, is *on the bit*. When the horse is on the bit, we have that great feeling that everything is possible and that the horse is comfortable. This position can be achieved and felt in hand, as well as in the saddle. With it, and with our other elements from our Molecular Mantra, our horse knows *where* to go, *how* to go, and the *physical* and *mental positions* that suit our dance. He is ready to *be one* with us. He is ready to be on the same level of consciousness as you.

how do we get the horse on the bit?

There are many ways to put a horse on the bit. Some approaches are softer than others. The softer methods are what we use.

It is very important that we prepare the horse properly before we ask him to be on the bit. That means that we longe him, we work him in hand, and we introduce the horse to the position progressively over time, perhaps a month or two. Every day we put him in the position and every day he enjoys being on the bit more and gets stronger; more energy is generated and transferred over and under the horse's now "rounded" frame.

As we know, being on the bit is both a *mental* and *physical* position. When the horse is comfortable in mind and in body, and when he enjoys being in the position we are requesting, then he will maintain it. When the horse *isn't* comfortable and *doesn't* enjoy it, he will fight it.

I remember as a young trainer longeing horses with two side reins, which I can now see created a lot of problems and resistance. Then we longed the horses too long, and they grew tired, trying to maintain the frame. I am not sure that the horses enjoyed being on the bit in this way. In retrospect, I feel that the combination of "rough" longeing (meaning with two side-reins and a forced position) and work in hand using a lot of outside rein was *not* a good training method. Because the horses were not enjoying the work, when we rode them and tried to put them on the bit, we encountered a lot of resistance and a lot of fight. Clearly now, those fights can be eliminated. It's all due to better preparation early in the horse's training.

I also remember how we used to seesaw on the horse's mouth, our hands spread apart and alternating right and left, in an effort to get the horse's head down. This was a mechanical way of achieving a position without thinking about the horse's mental well-being.

Today much horse training, in all disciplines, is still rough. In the jumping world, for example, there are some harsh methods and all kinds of bits and strings and stuff, such as draw reins. Any mechanism that forces the horse to be in the desired position is rough. And of course, something forced cannot be enjoyed. Force creates tension and resistance. We can't force someone to be happy. It is all in the right kind of preparation and after that, in the softness of the horse and his willingness to accept and then enjoy that position—on the bit, an essential condition for having the horse round and light.

assessing the horse's comfort when on the bit

When we join a gym and hire a personal trainer, he begins by evaluating our level of suppleness and what kind of physical shape we are in. He evaluates our muscle mass and maybe takes our heart rate or gives us a stress test to check for fitness. At the end he determines the right kind of cardio work and weight-lifting program in order to increase our physical and mental comfort as we pursue specific interests and even just regular day-to-day activities.

Similarly, as one example, the shoulder-in, whether on three or four tracks, is a test that we use to see what our horse *can* do, and to gauge what is comfortable for him and what is *not*. Another example is the haunches-in, as well as the combination of the two lateral exercises. How easily the horse can change from shoulder-in to haunches-in is an indication of his flexibility, suppleness, and comfort. The well-being of the horse is of the utmost importance, and we must always be very careful and never ask the horse to do something he cannot do because he lacks the physical and mental conditioning and preparation.

rethinking "natural"

The words "natural horsemanship" are used a lot in the equestrian world today and in related literature. The question is, what is actually natural for the trainer? For the horse?

When you put an anxious rider on a horse—which includes 95 percent of the riding population—the rider's physical reactions, based on fear, will be naturally wrong. The frightened rider leans forward, grips with the legs, pulls with the hands. This is what I call the "monkey relationship": If you put a monkey on a horse, it will lean forward, grip with its legs, and pull with its hands...because it is scared. *That* is natural.

All this natural stuff has to be rethought and re-understood from a different viewpoint, from a horse's viewpoint. Why does the horse behave a certain "way" about him in the first place? Why is he so nervous when he is in what most would call a "natural environment"? Because he is food for other animals. He needs to take care of himself—this is very important or he is dead.

Therefore, we need to make certain the horse feels comfortable, that he doesn't feel threatened by the position we put him in. We need to be sure that we are comfortable, as well. For when we are relaxed, we can then lean back, relax our legs, and give with our hands.

Forcing somebody to do something or act in a certain way is never good for him or her, physically or mentally, and is very likely *not* natural. In his books *Tug of War* and *Balancing Act*, Dr. Gerd Heuschmann proves, visually and with research, that forced training is not in the best interest of the horse. We have evidence that shows how many horses, across all disciplines, are drugged to ensure a certain performance during competition. It is terrible that the well-being of the horse is not the priority of many riders and trainers. Their priority is to win at all costs. There is no lightness to be found in such a scenario.

physically balanced, mentally balanced

All of us, human or horse, require a certain comfort, physically, in order to be mentally relaxed. If, for example, we have this very conversation with you standing on one foot on the edge of a cliff that drops 300 feet, you are not likely to listen to what I am saying. Physical balance is necessary for mental connection. Likewise, when the horse's balance is threatened, he is not listening to us—he reacts in fear. But when the horse is physically balanced, *then* we have a chance to establish a mental balance. We can help the horse stay balanced, generally, by *being* and *not* by *doing*. This gives the horse a chance to stay relaxed in the movement for which you are asking.

With in-hand work, we put the horse in a certain position, and we "touch him and let go," with the timing of the release being very important.

the alchemy of lightness

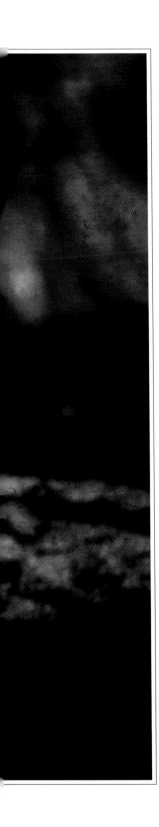

balance is strength

When I was seven years old my father decided that I should learn judo—the Japanese martial art that emphasizes the use of quick movement and leverage to throw an opponent. I was very lucky, for the man who taught me was a great master. He was a "seventh dan," one of the highest rankings attainable in judo, and the only Caucasian to have obtained that distinction at that time.

When I was young I was small and weak as a result of an illness. I remember it was the winter and very cold when I began to study the art. But I was very lucky to have a relationship with my teacher, even though he was 70-something years old and I was only seven-something years old.

Because I was not strong, I had to have technique that was impeccable. In judo, there are two different lineages of the art: *Kawaishi* and *Kodokan*. One is more physical and the other is more mental. While some who practice judo cannot rely on sheer mental force, they can use physical strength. For others, and for me, it is the opposite.

Everything in judo is about balancing, or actually, *un*balancing your opponent. When you push him, you want him to go toward you; if you pull him, you want him to go away from you. You always push or pull him to see which way he will go; which way the lack of balance will be greater. When the opponent's balance is better toward you, then you choose a movement that projects him to the outside. So, it is really a technique of balancing.

This experience helped me understand what we do with horses when we work in hand, and why. With in-hand work, we put the horse in a certain position, and we "touch him and let go," with the timing of the release being very important. When we hang on to the horse, we fight with him, and we cannot win a fight with such a big animal. Instead, as with the search for balance and imbalance in judo, when the horse is incorrect, we can correct him and bring him into balance very quickly when we know where to touch him and how to let go (release) at the right time. *Timing is a very important thing.* I learned that when I was a kid learning the art of judo. (I also learned a great respect for tradition, my master, and how one conducts oneself—I think it was a very good education.)

intuitively evaluating the horse's energy

When any two animals meet, there is some level of understanding—for example, we immediately assess another being's energy and personality to determine if they are friendly or not friendly using our intuition. When we meet a dog for the first time, let's say, and we want to put our hands forward to see if he will come toward us, we might not establish eye contact right away as it could cause the dog to jump on us or become aggressive. We have to read his energy and see if he is friendly. How do we know? Well, to tell the truth...I do not know, except to say that we engage in a "molecular reading" of sorts to determine what to do next.

For example, how do we know when to establish eye contact with another person? And sometimes we move away from someone and sometimes we move toward him or her. We are subconsciously or consciously evaluating their energy.

I believe that when we want to really *know* an animal or a person then we must sit with him and spend time with him. And if we sit down with him for a while with a "quiet mind"—a steady state of non-distractibility—and if we regulate our breath and become conscious of breathing together, then we figure out who the other being really is.

The ability to "forecast" a situation or occurrence has long been a subject of much interest. To study the phenomenon of what is known as having a "sixth sense" or intuitive perception (an inner "feeling" or hunch that comes to us before our mind has interpreted what we see or hear), researchers studied the record of success among a group of entrepreneurs. As a result, theories now contend that emotional attention directed toward an object (or being) of interest generates an identifiable and reliable psychophysiological response. During this process, our heart pattern becomes coherent (see p. 32) and our brain waves are consistent with those seen when we are in a meditative state,[70, 71] indicating that quieting the mind and controlling the breath are indeed the likely first steps to "intuitively" recognizing the horse's emotional and physical state.

learning through expression and molecular connection

As a clinician I have a short period of time to work with horses and riders, and I oftentimes do not have the luxury of systematically gymnasticizing each horse in the usual physical ways. This involves rethinking how horses learn.

The basic system of training that currently exists, and the one that most people are convinced is the only way, holds that repetition and association are the main routes to teaching the horse. Well, I do not think this is true. Yes, horses can learn through repetition. But are they able to learn in *another* way, without repetition and in a more sophisticated teacher-student relationship, as people do? True, we can teach people by simply repeating an exercise, but we can also explain what the exercise is first, and the complementary understanding of the task allows for faster learning.

A simple example can be had in the way we think about riding in general. Do we consider it an entirely *physical act* of *physically* repeated aids and the horse learning from his *physical* response to the repetition? Or do we send a *picture* to the horse, a *visualization* to help him *mentally* understand what we want as well as to provide a *visual guide* that we can then try to reproduce?

When we ride in the way of the former (purely physical), we probably consider our horse a "stupid animal," while when we ride in the way of the latter (incorporating visualization) we show that we understand that the animal can think, create, both receive and send mental pictures, and communicate with people as well as his fellow horses.

The general assumption about education is that most humans are probably unable to understand the nuances of a lesson, and so they have to be taught the "hard way" (repetition, repetition). Luckily, some believe in the benefits of "art school" or other alternative learning environments, and in these places, learning is different. There we learn ways of expressing ourselves in the course of absorbing the lesson—and it has been shown we are perfectly capable of acquiring new skills and knowledge in this way.

In the animal kingdom, education can work in the "art school" way. Horses have the ability to understand a lot more than the physical aspect of a lesson. This is why visualization is key to equestrian art: It leads to "molecular thinking"—an interaction on the mental and molecular level that allows the horse and the rider to understand his or her partner and feel as though they've become *one*.

learning seen through a scientific lens

Many horse people believe—and some even vehemently argue—that the horse's learning ability does not exist beyond basic associative learning (conditioning) and memory. Although much of how horses think can be explained by these mechanisms, it is critical for the well-being of horses to study whether they possess more advanced learning capability. In comparison with the amount of cognition research we've seen involving other animals, few studies into advanced equine learning have been completed—astounding considering the importance of horses to humans.

Fortunately, this is now changing as researchers design experiments that center on exploring more complex cognitive skills in equines. For example, the ability to categorize provides the basis to consider that horses have substantial higher cognitive function.[68] Dr. Evelyn Hanggi of the Equine Research Foundation in California has been conducting pioneering research to better understand how horses learn[73] and has shown how much more complex equine cognition may actually be.[16, 74] Her research in stimulus discrimination has shown, for example, that horses can tell the difference between objects, whether animate or inanimate. Furthermore, they can do so simply from looking at a picture.[16, 75] That is, it is very likely that our horse can pick us out from a line-up of mug shots! (Perhaps something we should remember?)

In fact, we are only now scratching the surface on the mystery of our equine companions' modes of feeling, mental processing, and learning. Cognition and perception in horses have often been misunderstood. Not only in the past but even today, people proclaim that horses react only by instinct, that they are just conditioned-response animals, that they lack advanced cognitive ability, and that they have poor visual capabilities (acuity, color vision, depth perception, for example). Dr. Hanggi suggests that horses possess a more sophisticated learning style than previously thought. Most recently and unexpected by many, horses have solved advanced cognitive challenges involving categorization learning and some degree of concept formation.[68]

Horses, like other mammals, are also capable of what Dr. Edwin Ray Guthrie[72] coined "one-trial learning." He believed that repetition in teaching, where a horse is forced to do the same thing over and over again, is not particularly necessary for learning to occur. He posited that a single pairing is all that may be needed for learning to happen and that maintenance of new learning does not require repeated associations and rewards.

An example of one-trial learning is as follows: When we eat something new and it tastes delicious, we learn to seek out that particular food. Similarly, a horse that has been given such *clarity of a cue* and provided with an experience associated with physical and mental comfort (reward or reinforcement) is likely to retain that memory. Learning in this way appears as something instant and effortless.

awareness of intent and being of two minds

It is possible for a horse to be aware of our *intent* (our determination to act in a certain way) before *we* are conscious of it. On the molecular level, transmission of intent occurs before our human consciousness is "up to date." I think that animals have the extraordinary ability to know "in the now" when things are *in the process* of happening. Their security, their safety, is based on that knowing. In the wild, when the horse is not aware of the mountain lion's proximity, he is eaten, gone. Therefore, he has developed a very important ability to be able to perceive another's intent. In our case, it is the "picture" in our head that he sees perhaps even before we do. He grabs it instantly.

This is why in my book *Dressage for the New Age* I talk about the "two minds": the mind *in the front*, which the horse can read, and the mind *in the back* that the horse cannot read. For instance, if we think that we would like to have the horse do a flying change in the corner after the short side, generally the horse does it immediately rather than waiting for the corner (of course, not all horses but most). This is why it is very important to "separate" our two minds. In order to perform the flying change as we wish, we must have our front mind say, "I will keep my normal canter," while in the back of our mind we know that we will be asking for a flying change. When we do not learn to separate our two minds, horses (generally) will execute what we want them to do *in the moment*.

This brings us back to why we must learn to *be* instead of *do*. For those people who have limited awareness of self and of energy, the horse definitely gets it first. When we are not present, we are not even part of the picture. In riders today, this is often the case...and that is why most horses look sleepy, or bored, or both.

*It is possible for the horse to be aware of
our intent before we are conscious of it.*

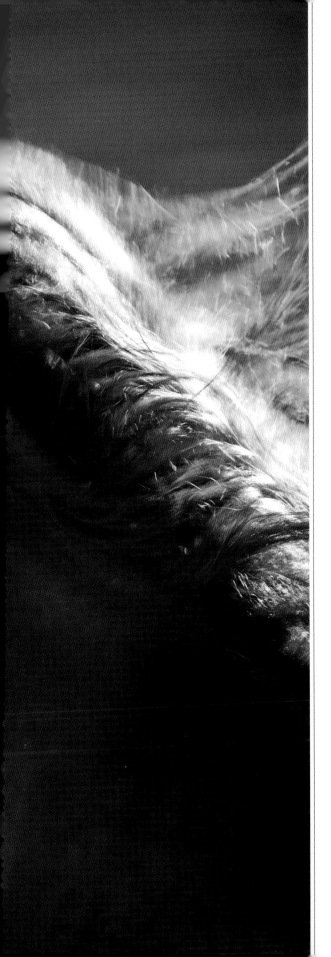

intent seen through a scientific lens

How can we even begin to explain intent and our horse's reaction to it? The concept of *non-local energy* is able to explain how a response is already happening even *before* we are consciously aware of it. Dr. Benjamin Libet, a pioneering scientist in the realm of human consciousness, discovered that our consciousness projects itself backward in time—that is, the brain is convinced that it became aware of an action *before* it occurred, while in reality it became aware of the action a half-second later. Dr. Libet conducted a series of experiments where he determined the exact point at which the brain registered a sensation on the skin. He measured when the skin became aware of the sensation and when the brain did. This led to the discovery of the "half-second delay" mentioned above.

Dr. Libet's experiments also measured the difference in time from the activation of our brain to move our arm to the point where we say, "I am moving my arm." The Danish science writer Tor Norretranders explains Libet's work by saying, "The show starts *before* we decide it should! An act is initiated before we decide to perform it!" [76] And the horse, as a prey animal that evolved to survive in the wild, is in tune to the act, whatever it may be, when it is initiated—so that means before we have consciously decided to perform it.

Check-In

Use these prompts to review the ideas we've discussed so far:

1

How is the horse our teacher?

2

*Has being with and riding horses "healed"
you in some way? How?*

3

*Describe the elements necessary for the horse's
comfort and that lead to molecular change.*

4

*How is our own clarity of vision important
to our horse?*

chapter 4

Creating Lightness

when the artist becomes the art

The possibility of *lightness* is easy and available to us. It is one where the artist's responsibility is to embrace the idea that *simplicity is key*. As we have discussed, it is in the French classical tradition that we find a blueprint for lightness originating from the rider that results in *descente de main et de jambes*. In this manner, the ideal is characterized by the absence of any unnecessary force, which then results in a lightness of the horse and a lightness of the rider's hands and legs.

One simple responsibility that we share is that of being open to the possibility that we are both *the creators of* and *part of the creation that is* the "molecular relationship," the union with the horse leading to oneness. In us, a desire to learn must also be a willingness to change deeply.

Lightness is a state of mind in which the horse and the rider are one.

Lightness is a state of mind in which the horse and the rider are one. For the rider this entails *descente de main et de jambes*—the rider relaxes the hands until it feels as if he or she has no hands and relaxes the legs until it feels as if he or she has no legs. In other words, the rider learns *to be* and ceases *to do*, no longer enacting the physical and allowing the horse to carry on with specific movements on his own. This is when the molecular relationship between rider and horse qualifies as lightness.

Lightness is *légèreté* in French, which actually means that the horse moves as if he is on his own and without the rider interfering. There is a total absence of force. Lightness comes from the rider's attitude, both physical and mental— something very far from the hard and destructive half-halts often seen in the competitive dressage arena.

Again, ultimately, it is not *what we do* but *who we are*. When we are in the present moment and fully available, when we are in the same "frequency" with another person or animal (see p. 35), then our fellow creature will be at ease with us.

When lightness is achieved, the horse moves as if on his own, without the rider interfering.

simple goals for the rider

I have two simple wishes for every rider:

1

*I want the rider not to upset the horse,
physically or mentally. What could upset
him physically and mentally? All the
gesticulations and movements that are
not only unnecessary, but actually work
against the horse. Therefore, 95 percent of
the rider's time should be spent ensuring
that he or she does not upset the horse.*

2

*I want the rider to have clarity of
mind. The rider needs to be as clear as
possible in his or her visualization and
communication so the horse is able to
know what is desired of him.*

The synthesis of these two elements—not upsetting the horse and clarity
of mind—produces the very great feeling on horseback that we desire.

The horse's happiness must be the rider's primary concern. Love is unconditional. We must also understand that loving is *not necessarily allowing all
behaviors*. Loving our horse is to educate that horse for his own happiness.
When we give everything to a child, for example, there is no discipline.
Ultimately, the child without discipline will not be happy. Like a child,
a horse is not happy if he does not know his limits, his own boundaries.

In addition, the horse's right to self-expression must be considered. After
learning basic dressage, some horses may prefer expressing themselves via
a different discipline, like jumping or eventing or simply pleasure riding.
The rider is somebody who, as I have said in all my books, dedicates his or
her life to the training of horses while making sure that their well-being
is the highest priority. We must always enjoy the little things and not get
caught up in a competitive agenda or focus only on attaining an outcome.

preparing to facilitate the "molecular relationship"

The space in which you can be *receptive to* and *communicate with* your horse only exists when you are *one with yourself*—calm and centered. *Centering* is a process that helps us manage our energy, focus on our inner strength and calm and ignore outside intrusions. People who practice martial arts *center* themselves, as do those who pursue yoga and those who meditate. Some religious groups center themselves before or during worship or prayer—*Merkabah*, for example, in the Jewish religion, offers a great technique of centering...and we all have rituals. Sometimes these centering rituals are religious in nature, but they don't have to be—for example, comedians, dancers, singers, and athletes all have their own ways of centering before they perform.

We must learn that silence is okay. We must feel that contemplation is okay. We must feel that what many call "emptiness" is okay. This means we don't need stimulation, we don't need to multitask, we don't need to be agitated, we don't need to be anxious. We don't need to do well or have expectations we must meet. It is when we have a state of "non-expectation" that we can be calm and peaceful inside. And it is at this moment that we can start to feel.

centering and consciousness seen through a scientific lens

There are deliberate actions we can take in our day-to-day interactions with our horse that can affect us in every way, on a cellular level. Every word we speak, every action we take throughout the day, causes a reaction in our genes.

Science is finally catching up to where spirituality has been for thousands of years: The Buddha urged us to maintain a calm state of "desireless" attention to the present moment, reminding us that, "We are what we think. All that we are arises with our thoughts. With our thoughts, we make the world."[3] *Consciousness* is customarily defined in terms of "the quality or state of being aware, especially within oneself...the state or fact of being conscious of an external event, object, state or fact...awareness."[77] And Ernest László's research has shown that meditation is one way that we can harness our ability to deliberately regulate brain waves, heart rhythm,

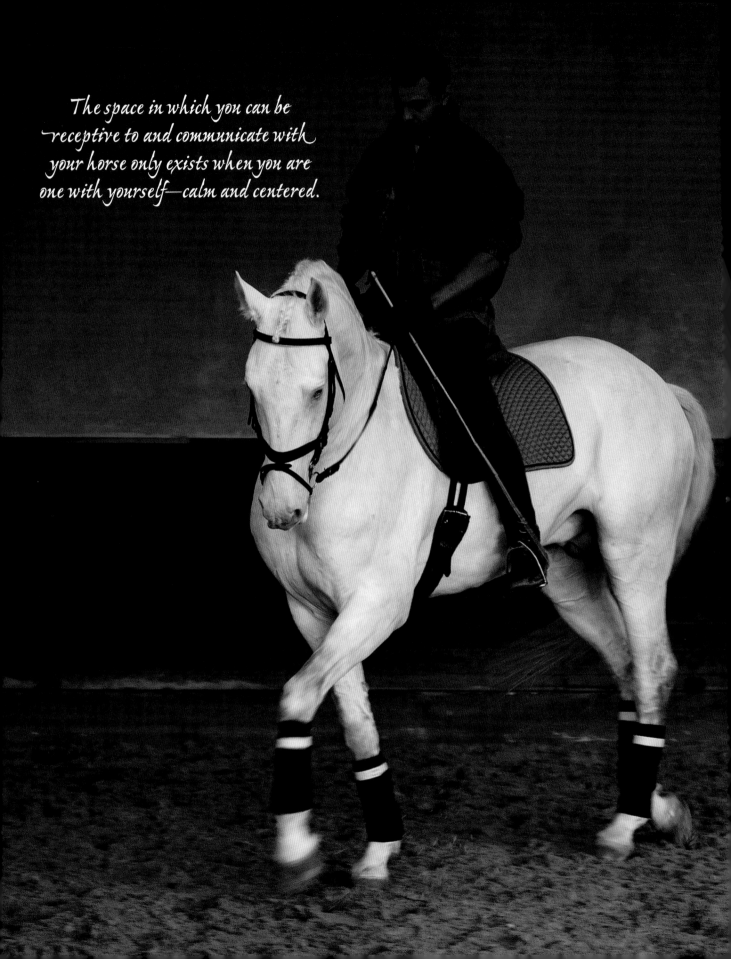

*The space in which you can be
receptive to and communicate with
your horse only exists when you are
one with yourself—calm and centered.*

and other variables to achieve states of altered consciousness[43]—that is, *become centered*.

As mentioned previously in this book, a series of experiments using positron emission tomography (PET) scans and brain wave recordings to study the regions of the brain have shown us what occurs in the brain while we meditate. Experienced meditators showed brain waves that correspond to states of focused attention, improved memory, and enhanced learning.[21] They also had more brain activity in areas linked to positive emotions, like happiness. Monks who spent the most years meditating showed the most evidence of such brain changes.[78] Meditative techniques seem to, in effect, prepare us mentally and physically for communion with the horse. It would also appear that the more often we practice, the more our mind and body will reflect our inner state of *quiet being*—and the better our horsemanship will then be down the road.

what can happen molecularly in three days

I often work with riders and their horses over the course of three days in a clinic scenario. The morning of the first day I meet each horse, and more importantly, I evaluate the quality of the relationship each horse has with his rider while they are on the longe line. At this time I must detect any "missing parts" or misunderstandings between them.

I then need to give or reinforce certain information with the horses in mind—for example, forward motion needs to be established on the longe line and their level of suppleness is determined through work in hand. In both those processes I determine how willing or not the horses are to "dance." The assessment on the longe and in hand will give me a pretty good understanding of what I need to fix and what lessons need to carry through to later work under saddle, when I want to just *be* and not *do*.

The afternoon of the first day I discuss my morning observations with the riders and work with them to convey the same message to the horses that I determined necessary during the morning assessment—in essence, the invitation to share in an intermolecular energy exchange. Usually, I am teaching the riders to do less and not to disturb their horses. I am inviting them to center themselves and open their mind to the possibility of attaining the feeling they desire by simply *allowing* the horse to perform movements, rather than *making* him.

The morning of the second day, if the riders are much calmer, more relaxed, then the horses already better understand what will be asked of them. For me, in terms of the horses, the second day is just to confirm the basic program explored the day prior in search of the means of *molecular change* in them, and in me *with* them. By now, the riders will have seen this change occurring, now twice, and they will start to believe in the possibility and will be more able to imagine that they, too, can experience it.

The third day of a clinic is very easy for me and the horses. The *transmutation*—our conversion from old into new, from two into one—has already happened at both the body and mind level. The horses have assimilated all the changes noted as necessary on day one, and they start to be confirmed. The riders now have seen this process happen between me and their horse three times and are, most of the time, now open to experience what has become a different being.

feeling is key

The transmutation I've mentioned throughout this book occurs when we are able to create *what we want* out of *what we have*. If we are able to *have the feeling* and to *keep the feeling* of what we want, then we are in the process of *creating* exactly what we want. The key is we not only *see* it, we *feel* it. When we can *feel* what we want, we can *feel* our horse as we want him in the walk, the canter, the piaffe, the passage.

The problem arises when we focus on the obstacle between what we have now and what we want. Because we focus on the obstacle—we see it, we feel it—what do we create? We create the obstacle!

Any time we are able to sustain a vision and feeling then guess what? We are creating it! And that is exactly what I do with horses. I cannot train a horse in three days, but I *see* and I *feel* the changes I want in the horse and in our relationship. This is an act of creation. To sustain it, I must remain at the same level of consciousness and practice, each day that follows.

Let me share a story: When I was in Portugal, I bought a young horse. His name was Dom Pasquale. By this time, I had done a little bit of everything, but I had never trained a horse to Grand Prix. I realized that alone, I could not do it. But, I also knew someone close by, Mestre Nuno Oliveira, who had done it many times. I understood that if I wanted to do it, I needed to know what he knew. In order to know, in effect, I needed to *be* him because of what he knew. Therefore, for many sessions I was not *me* riding Dom Pasquale, I was *Mestre Oliveira* riding Dom Pasquale. And I felt very different because I had assumed the feeling of the complete picture and all that I knew, he knew.

The result was that in basically nine months, Pasquale was able to do every part of the Grand Prix test.

feeling seen through a scientific lens

The role and impact of *feeling* in our ability to create experiences with our horse is key. Experiments conducted in the late twentieth century have shown that it is human feeling and emotion that affect the "stuff" our reality is made of—it is our inner language that changes the atoms, electrons, and photons of the outer world. Note that this is not about the actual words we utter but about the feeling that they create within us. It is the language of emotion that speaks to the "quantum forces" of the universe. It should also be noted that the word "emotion" is seen more readily referenced in scientific material than the word "feeling." While these words are similar, science makes a distinction between them: The book *Theories of Emotion Psychology* describes *emotions* as involving a complex experience of an individual's state of mind as it interacts with biochemical and environmental influences, while *feeling* reflects composite perceptions about things, situations, or people.

"There's a subtle yet powerful difference between working toward a result and thinking and feeling toward it."

Gregg Braden, Author of *The Divine Matrix*

Modern science has discovered that through each emotion we experience in our body, we also undergo chemical changes—for example, blood pH (the balance of acid and alkaline) and hormone levels actually mirror our feelings.[3, 81] In the pages ahead, I mention a few studies where scientists continue to decode the precise pathways by which changes in human consciousness produce changes in the human body.[3] Through the "positive" experiences of love, compassion, and forgiveness we possess the power to affirm or deny our existence, and that of other beings, at each moment of every day. The same emotion that gives us such power *within* our body extends this force into the quantum "field" *beyond* our body, allowing us to connect to other beings and to something even greater than ourselves.

how feelings affect our dna

If *feeling* is key to the transmutation that occurs with our horses in the path to lightness, how is it that it occurs, on a molecular level? As mentioned, there is a robust link between human emotion and the way our cells function in our body.[81] During the 1990s, scientists working with the United States Army investigated whether or not the power of our feelings affected living cells, specifically DNA. A 1993 study reported in the journal *Advances* documents how the army performed experiments to determine precisely whether the connection between emotions and DNA continues following a separation, and if so, at what distance (see Theory 1 below).[82] Two examples of related experiments and their findings follow to show just how this occurs and the impact it has both on our own body and on other beings.

theory 1: our feelings can affect other living things at a distance

A sample of DNA was collected from the inside a number of volunteers' mouths and taken to another room several hundred feet away in the same building. Each study participant was then shown a series of video images in order to generate a spectrum of genuine states of emotion within a brief period of time. The pictures selected ranged from comedy to graphic wartime footage.

In the other room, the DNA samples were measured electronically to see if they responded to the emotions of the individuals they came from. When a donor experienced emotional "peaks" and "dips," his cells and DNA showed a powerful electrical response at the *same instant in time*. Although the donor and his DNA sample were clearly separated, the DNA acted as if it was still physically connected to his body. Researchers continued to explore this phenomenon by increasing the distances between the donor and the DNA. At one point, a span of 350 miles separated the study participant and his cells.

If the donor is experiencing emotions within his or her body and the DNA is responding to those emotions, then something must be traveling between them that allows the emotion to get from one place to the other, right? The results of this experiment suggest three things:

1

*A previously unrecognized form of energy
exists between living tissues.*

2

*Human emotion has a direct influence on
living DNA and cells.*

3

*DNA communicates through a field of energy, and
distance appears to be of no consequence with
regard to the effect. (Whether we're in the same
room with our DNA or separated by distances
of hundreds of miles, we're still connected to its
molecules, and the effect is the same.)*

Review my introduction to the "Web of Connection," beginning on p. 12, and consider what such research suggests in terms of how we ultimately communicate with our horse.

theory 2: the heart radiates a powerful energy field

The key to lightness may reside in the place in our body where emotion and feeling seem to originate—the human heart. As touched upon on p. 47, our heart produces electricity. Our body and that of the horse produce energy. One of the most significant findings reported by the Institute of HeartMath is the documentation of the field of energy that surrounds the heart and extends beyond the body—in humans and in horses.[13] Researchers were interested in exploring the impact of various emotions on heart rhythm and the energy it emits, and its effect on human DNA.

Using special techniques that analyze the DNA, both chemically and visually, researchers found that human emotions changed the shape of DNA. Without physically touching it or doing anything other than creating precise feelings in their body, study participants were able to influence DNA molecules in a beaker. So...human emotion has a direct effect on DNA, which in turn directly impacts the "stuff" our world is made of. This is the beginning of a kind of technology—an *inner technology* that does more than simply tell us we can have an effect on our body and our world. The DNA in our body gives us access to the field of energy that connects our universe, and *feeling* is the key to tapping into that field.

> *"Feeling is the language that 'speaks' to the Divine Matrix [the quantum 'field']. Feel as though your goal is accomplished and your prayer is already answered."*

—Gregg Braden, *The Divine Matrix*

the role of energy in creating lightness

The language of energy is simple. There exist two different kinds of energy generated by the two different kinds of emotions we discussed earlier in the book: energy created by fear and energy created by love. Nervous energy and calm energy. We experience nervous energy when engaged with an upset horse, and calm energy when around a happy horse.

How do we keep an unlimited supply of the right kind of energy? The secret is in centering (see p. 75), feeling the positive emotions that make us and others happy, and then sharing it. Giving out calm energy makes *us* stronger and more available all the time. It is a choice. Helping others to be stronger and healthier will strengthen and heal us. Those who are strong and healthy who do not heal, or do not share their gift, can make themselves sick. *Energy must flow*...its movement will give us peace and joy. If we share our strong energy, we will never lack of it.

Consider engaging in random acts of kindness. Feel you are part of the beauty of the world, the abundance and joy that is yours to be had. This energy will flow through you and radiate outward.

using energy to overcome resistances

To bypass uneasiness or physical resistance ("blocks") in the horse, we need to use our energy. This should be considered a kind of "healing" process where the chakras (the points of spiritual and physical energy in the human body) are "open" and transmitting energy to the horse. We want to strike a balance between energizing and relaxing the horse in order to create change in his mind, helping him realize he *can* perform the movement we request. Our energy is the key here: When the horse has little or no energy due to resistance, he cannot perform; however, when we provide the energy, when we share it with him from our body and mind, we can help him help himself, and do so correctly. Use of our energy is really fundamental to our work with the horse.

For those of us who might find these ideas new, engaging in yoga practice can help facilitate our ability to create awareness of and modulate our energy. Once developed, this awareness and confidence makes it much easier to help the horse overcome any energetic resistance.

energy's effect seen through a scientific lens

Research points to the power of energy, the impact our emotions have on energy, and energy's effect on all things that surround us, including our horses. When we think of energy, we typically imagine it being generated in one place and then somehow transmitted or conveyed to another, which would take time, even if only a little. The key in the experiment measuring human emotion's impact on DNA described on p. 80, however, was that an atomic clock (accurate to one second in one million years) showed that *no time elapsed* between generation of feeling and the change in DNA *in a separate room*. The effect of energy in both places was simultaneous because in the quantum "field," the study subject and his DNA were part of the same energy "pattern," and the information from one was already present with the other: *They were already connected*. The energy from the study subject's emotions *never traveled anywhere*, because *it was already everywhere*.[84]

Energy must flow...

its movement will give us

peace and joy.

We are in communication with DNA—ours and that of other beings—through our emotions. Whether that DNA is in our body or separated by miles, the effect is still the same and can be explained by the science of *non-local energy* (see p. 69). Intermolecular energy exchange is happening all the time. It does not have to travel from one point to another. This means that the *energy exchange* that leads to *molecular change* between us and the horse is instant...it is already happening.

As well as beings of matter, we are beings of energy. As we've discussed, there is an electromagnetic component to every living being. The energy flows in neurons and genes that interact with each other.[4] Between 1993 and 2000, a series of extraordinary experiments demonstrated the existence of an underlying field of energy.[4] The first experiment, called the "DNA Phantom Effect," suggests that human DNA directly affects the physical world.[85] Researchers concluded that there exists a type of energy previously undiscovered and that DNA/cells influence matter through this form of energy. The experiment validated the claim that we impact the world around us via our energy by showing how human DNA has a direct effect on the vibration of light.[86]

The human body is in essence an "electric generator" whose primary purpose is the transference of energy.[87] Electromagnetic fields are both generated by and have an effect on our body, as well as in all other living things around us.[88] A series of experiments by French doctor Jacques Beneviste demonstrated the effects of electromagnetic fields in a novel way. He used the heart as his subject. The compound known as *histamine* increases heart rate. Rather than administering histamine itself to view its effects, Beneviste simply exposed a beating heart to the *electrical frequency* of the histamine molecule, and by doing so, speeded up the rate of heart muscle contraction. Next he exposed the same heart to the electrical signature of *atropine*, which *decreases* heart rate, and found it reduced the flow of blood in the coronary arteries, just as the actual administration of the organic compound would have done.[89] He was able to show how just the electromagnetic frequencies of the compounds had the same effect as the compounds themselves.[90]

Research has shown that electromagnetic fields have a measurable effect on other life forms, such as water and plants. Bernard Grad, Ph.D., of McGill University, experimented with "healers" who performed a "laying on of hands" on a number of water samples (a "blessing," as some might call it). These water samples, as well as control samples, were then used for germinating plant seeds. Dr. Grad found that those seeds that were watered with the "blessed" water grew significantly faster and larger than those that were not. He conducted the same experiment using patients diagnosed with psychotic depression to "bless" the water samples, and in this case, Dr. Grad found that the plants receiving the "blessed" water fared poorly.[91]

It seems the evidence is mounting that the energy our bodies and minds generate impacts that which surrounds us, and it is in the control of that energy that we may achieve union with the horse with ease, with pleasure, with joy.

physical elements necessary to facilitate *molecular change*

The physical attitude of the rider is an important component in the search for lightness.

First, we must position our body properly in relation to the horse's. The physical position should be such that it enables the kind of *mental communication* I mentioned earlier in the book (see p. 17). I call this "assuming the right attitudes": both physical and mental.

Well, how do we do this? We begin with relaxation. The rider should sit in the saddle in a way that allows the positioning of *his or her* center of gravity closer to *the horse's* center of gravity, which is "between" the rider's knees. This center of gravity changes a little bit in the course of riding, but not much. The rider should sit toward the *front part of the saddle* and on the *back of the seat bones*. The rider's legs should be totally relaxed and stretched down, the body very straight, as if someone suspended above were pulling a hair on the top of the rider's head straight up.

The ideal is to be in a position where we can move easily with the body of the horse as he moves, without any tenseness. I recommend *simplicity* in finding our seat. Sit how a six-year-old child naturally sits on a pony—relaxed, joyful, and in a perfect position without trying too hard.

How does this position support and encourage the intermolecular energy exchange we desire in order to attain lightness?

We are examining the idea of *position* versus that of *action*. Position refers to the orientation of our body and the body of the horse in order to create lightness. The two bodies must be in harmony. Horse and rider must feel that they *can* become one— without interference.

It is true that as we ride we put our body in certain positions: We lean back, move our leg back, bring our outside hand higher, play with our fingers, make the inside rein shorter. All these are positions. Now, that *does not* imply that we have to then push with the seat, bang with the leg, or pull on the rein. Those are *actions*, not positions. Positions begin as *passive* and later they can become "giving."

We sometimes see trainers rely on "big" actions. They think they need big actions in order to make the horse understand and react. We have to believe that very little is needed for what we want to do with our horse. When we do not believe this, then we automatically ride using *action* instead of *position*. In actuality, *very little* is needed to become one with the horse. When the rider starts to feel and believe that "less is more," he or she has taken a major step in understanding lightness.

by the "tips of the fingers"

The tips of the rider's fingers are a fundamental component to lightness. I use the idea of holding the reins only with the "tips of the fingers" because it makes it impossible for the rider to be strong, to pull, or to force. When we use only the tips of our fingers—holding the reins like they are "dirty," like something we do not want to touch—then we have the feeling that we cannot pull on or brace against the horse.

In a sense, this is exactly what the reins should be—something we don't want to touch unless we have to. The length of the reins allows the horse to find his own correct position and when he does, there should be absolutely no contact, only the weight of the reins—no force, no compression. Now obviously, this concept occurs as a progression with the horse. He needs to gain an understanding of holding himself in self-carriage through work on the longe and in hand.

*If we ride the horse lightly,
he will be light with us—
as light as we want him.*

Ideally, when we pick up the reins with the tips of our fingers the horse stays in the same position and replicates the contact that we give him. When we start with the slightest contact on the reins with our fingers, then he will answer with lightness. The result of our not pulling, not compressing, is that the horse will stay in self-carriage. Note, of course, that we do need to create the proper energy to keep him there.

The reason that riding by the "tips of the fingers" works is that the horse mirrors what we do to him. If we ride him strongly, he will be strong with us. If we ride him lightly, he will be light with us—as light as we want him. The limit of lightness is the weight of the reins and leather. That gives us the feeling that we have exactly what we want and nothing more.

This is the philosophy I apply to every aspect of my life. Most people, they pull, and then they pull harder. But there is no pulling necessary...it is never a pulling in the quest for lightness. It is about the hand that does not move. It is a hand that gives.

"Tip-of-the-finger" lightness is what determines our relationship with the horse. It is just a refinement of the use of the reins. We position the horse and then we have to be as light as we can with our hands. Handling the reins in this way prevents us from being too strong—it is amazing how we might *think* we need to be strong, even when we don't have to be. We must notice how horses respond so well to young children...it is because the children are not strong, and therefore, the horse is never strong with them.

mental elements necessary to facilitate *molecular change*

The rider's mental attitude is very important. The mind of the person, like the person's body, must be relaxed, and the person must know what he/she wants to do so that the horse can then know what the "dance" is about. We must go back to the original Molecular Mantra I described on pp. 16 and 17: *Direction, Rhythm, Bend, Lightness*. Providing these four elements, in order, allows the horse to understand what we want to do with him.

When we are in the physical and mental attitude I have described here, we are truly with the horse, and we are in a wonderful space. After that, we need to know our goals. When our goal is to have lightness, then we have to do less every time we repeat a movement: less with our hands, less with our legs, less mechanically, and less physically. We need to become more aware of a constant "being with" attitude with the body and the mind.

how to use our breath when with the horse

When on the horse especially, and also when we work in hand or when we are longeing, we must think about breathing *out*. Breathing *out* is what we have to become conscious of…breathing *in* is an automatic thing. Breathing *out* is what we need to take charge of. Each time we are tight, tense, and afraid, we stop breathing, and then so does our horse. Therefore, it is very important to continue breathing, to be conscious of our breathing and the breathing of the horse, and to be conscious of breathing together. That breathing is going to help us relax and stay present and consistent in what we want to do in the saddle.

power in mindfulness of breath seen through a scientific lens

One of the ways to understand when our body relaxes, and feel it when we are on our horse, is to become conscious of our breathing. For centuries humankind has known that when we are aware of our breathing, we are aware of our state of relaxation.[92, 93] Basic techniques of meditation always start with breathing because it helps us feel where there are *physical* or *mental* tensions. Recent scientific advances indicate that *slow breathing*, often observed in people during mediation or prayer, has powerful effects on the body.[94, 95] For example, psychiatrist Dr. Paul M. Lehrer has been investigating how to harness *power reflexes* via slow breathing for enhanced health and wellness. He assessed Zen monks during their usual meditative practice and discovered something fascinating: Slow breathing, sometimes only one to three breaths per minute, affected thermoregulatory properties in the body. By the end of their meditation, the monks' robes were drenched in sweat…and this after meditating atop a mountain on an ice-cold day![95] Italian researcher Luciano Bernardi found that nuns, when practicing their rosary prayer, naturally breathed around six breaths per minute. This rate of respiration also produced powerful reflexes in the body, this time with major implications on focus, resilience, and enhanced performance.[96]

The simple act of changing our own breathing has the potential of affecting our horse, and everything else that interacts in our environment.

Research conducted by research physicist Dr. Robert Beck illustrates the mechanisms involved in the process of changing our own physiological state with the potential of affecting our horse. Dr. Beck noticed that charts of the oscillations of the earth's own magnetic frequencies resembled the brain-wave pattern readouts of some humans. The earth usually resonates at 7.8 Hz, and his research found that individuals who practiced breathing techniques for healing (such as Amazonian shamans, Hawaiian kahunas, Christian faith healers, Buddhist lamas, and Indian yogis) had brain-wave frequencies that resonated very closely to the earth's frequency, at 7.83Hz, and many times actually beat in phase with the earth's signal. Those who carefully manage their breath seem to tap into a universal communication frequency.[102] They are "in sync"— connected to something greater than themselves.

It has become apparent that we can elicit powerful changes in our body simply by being aware and adjusting our breathing. And there's more! Feelings of joy and happiness, which correspond to consistent breathing rates, elicit coherent heart patterns[13] that are associated with health[97-99] and improved mental clarity (see p. 32 for more on heart coherence).[92, 100, 101] Our breath is power!

the story of the bubble and the golden ball

Earlier in this book I described the "bubble" of space we occupy in order to feel that oneness is available to us. It is a space that we have to access to truly focus. I think that all performers find their way into the bubble when they prepare to take the stage of the theatre or create music. In that space, everything is "golden"—favorable.

A long time ago someone gave me a book to read; it was about creating a "cloud" or "bubble" around oneself. It tells us to create a cloud of thousands of little sparkles...golden sparkles. We need to make it very precise and very golden and be intense in our visualization. The whole body is sur-rounded by that golden, sparkly bubble. When we can let ourselves go and create the bubble as a playful child might, then the whole self *changes* (we can say it is a *molecular change*).

The "Golden Ball" is a meditation technique I adapted to help in our pur-suit of equestrian art. It is a parallel exercise to the bubble visualization, or something that gets very close to it.

1

Imagine a ball perhaps the size of a ping-pong ball, and it's all brilliant...brilliantly gold and sparkling. When all is well, the ball is located in your lower chakras, below your naval and near the base of your spine (the energy centers associated with relationships, awareness of others, and physical vitality). When you do not know where the ball is, when you do not sense it glowing at your base, then that ball is in your throat. The throat is generally where all fear and anxiety are concentrated, as well as anger.

2

As in the idea of the sparkling bubble (see p. 92), you can now turn your fear, anxiety, and anger into a game, into child's play. Imagine that golden ball stuck in your throat. You cannot control the ball; the only thing you can control is your breathing. You can breathe down the ball. Breathe and imagine that golden ball going from your throat down your spine and traveling to your lower chakras. Feel a sort of silly smile on your face as this happens. There is a sense of contentment, a feeling of peace as you breathe the ball down. If something happens and you get scared or disturbed or distracted, that ball comes right back up, stuck in your throat.

3

Some days the ball goes down very easily; some days the ball is stuck. The more practice you have, the easier it is to breathe that ball down and keep it down. For example, start by sitting on the horse at a halt and practice keeping the ball down. Then try to keep the ball down at the walk. Walk around, breathe the ball down, and again get that silly smile on your face.

4

Once you are able to consistently breathe that ball down and keep it down, then imagine a ray of light extending into your body. Meditative traditions often visualize the ray of light as a column of energy extending from the top of your head, but for riding purposes, I describe the big ray of light as shining into your chest. Imagine this very bright, golden light entering your torso and going down your spine, landing on that beautiful golden ball.

Then again, in a playful way, see that light touch the golden ball and add to it—making it bigger. The ball gets bigger and bigger as the ray of light flows to it until it is no longer encapsulated by your body, but instead it encapsulates you and your horse. When you and your horse are surrounded by this golden, sparkling bubble, which is steadily growing from that ray of light shining into your chest, you do not have a single riding problem. You have achieved oneness.

When you and your horse are one, you are immersed in that feeling you have when you love somebody. You can hold that feeling and take your bubble with you when you get off your horse. You can put your bubble around other people, other creatures. Whichever church you go to, whichever quiet place of peace you rely on, be it building or forest or river, can help you channel that ray of light and continue to make your golden bubble bigger. Soon you can put your whole town in it. And then your country. You can even dare to imagine world peace inside your bubble—it just depends on the size of the bubble you have.

The feeling we can experience when we are with our horse in the bubble is extraordinary. When we are in that space, *nothing* can touch us. In summary, to get there, we must practice:

- Locating the golden ball.

- Breathing the ball down our spine to our lower chakras.

- Visualizing the ray of light beaming in through our chest, down our spine, and making the ball bigger until it becomes a sparkling bubble that surrounds us and our horse.

- Learning to stay as long as we can in that state...in that bubble.

The "Golden Ball" exercise requires practice. But once we've mastered it, we can create movement within it and be in complete harmony with our horse. We can create an extraordinary feeling of becoming one with another being and dancing as one—perhaps the most God-like feeling that I know. The result is an amplification of purity and intent as you partner with the horse. And this *intent* is fundamentally important for *molecular change.*

"take care of your onions"

In French we have a saying, *occupe-toi de tes oignons* ("take care of your onions.") In English we say, "take care of your business." We all have to take care of something important—improvement of self.

How do we go about peeling an onion? Onions are pungent, although some of them are sweeter than others. We all have difficulty in the peeling process...lots of crying...lots of making faces as we turn away. It's not always comfortable. But every morning we have to peel our onion. We have to look at ourselves and take another layer off. We need to open up to get closer to the center. We can do this slowly over time or more quickly.

The feeling we can experience when we are with our horse in the "bubble" is extraordinary—in that space, nothing can touch us.

We have to peel our onion all our life, over and over again, in order to train our ego, to strip back the layers of fear. We feel so much better with a "slimmer" ego. Then the crying is not so painful. We feel better when we are filled with a sweet sense of love and passion.

As we discussed on p. 35, we have to consciously choose between two emotions in life: *love* and *fear*. Let us be compassionate to ourselves; let us peel our onion with openness and shed layer after layer as we learn to change. Sometimes we can even learn to enjoy onion-peeling.

Check-In

Use these prompts to review the ideas we've discussed so far:

1
Describe "lightness" in the rider.

2
Explain how descent de main et de jambes is key in cultivating lightness.

3
How does "feeling" affect the intermolecular energy exchange between rider and horse?

4
Describe how our breath has the power to affect the process of transmutation.

the alchemy of lightness

chapter 5

Change Our Consciousness to Change Our Riding

where do we begin?

Changing our level of consciousness is the first
important step to having a clear understanding and
vision of our goal—riding in lightness. Many people
have little or no vision of what they want to attain,
so they often work backward or start by doing the
opposite of what the goal requires.

When our ideal is the image of a horse in *descente de main et de jambes* (see p. 17), then we have to *start* with something very light. As mentioned in the previous chapter, we want the reins to be held in the tips of our fingers (see p. 88). When the goal is lightness, it is better to *start light* than to begin with closed hands that are pulling on the horse. Likewise, if we want to ride with very little leg, it is better to start by relaxing our legs versus kicking our horse at every stride.

Our vision is about being conscious of our goals, as clear as we can be...as clear as our "knowledge" allows us to be. *Knowledge on horseback is feeling.* And when we are clear in knowing what we want, the horse will enjoy doing what we want.

clarity of vision seen through a scientific lens

Clarity of vision is a powerful ingredient in the recipe to create *molecular change*. Stanford University research psychologist Dr. Carol Dweck performed a study focused on seventh grade students and their math scores that helps illustrate how clarity of vision works.

Dr. Dweck found that the beliefs that students held regarding their own intelligence level had a direct effect on their performance. Some students believed that "intelligence" is a fixed and unchanging predetermined characteristic, like height. Others believed that intelligence can grow and develop, like a plant. Dr. Dweck compared the math scores of the two groups of students over the course of the following two years and found that students who believed that intelligence can grow and develop improved their math scores.

To test the impact of visualization on performance, Dr. Dweck then took a group of 100 seventh graders who were all performing badly in math and divided them, at random, into two groups. The first group received instruction in good study skills. The second group received more elaborate information that included the ways our brain grows and forms new neural connections when confronted with novelty and challenge. These students were educated in how the brain makes neural connections that, over time, make us smarter. Dr. Dweck reported that then, when students "worked hard in school, they actually *visualized* how their brain was growing."[103] At the end of the semester, those students who had received the "mini-course" in neuroscience had significantly better math grades than the other group.

the alchemy of lightness

A 2007 Harvard study examined the effects of *perception on outcome* among a volunteer sample of 84 hotel maids who were divided into two groups. One group was presented with the idea that their work qualified as good exercise while the other group was not. Over the next thirty days the changes recorded in the bodies of the women who been told their work was a form of exercise were significant—they lost an average of two pounds and lowered their blood pressure by almost 10 percent.[104] Bodily changes occurred in these women because they *perceived* themselves as getting a considerable amount of exercise.

What we imagine, we can create. What we believe is happening shapes our reality. What we visualize for our riding, for our horse, is well within reach.

the "lightness" state of mind

When we are *mindful*, our mind is absorbed by what we are doing, step by step, and we are entirely *present* (in the moment). I think that today the problem is that people are in a state of "senses overload." They are driving and texting at the same time, checking Facebook and at the same time watching television. This overload of sensation destroys a person's ability to be present mentally.

Mindfulness is integral to riding in lightness. To be in communication, to be in a relationship, to achieve oneness, it is all-important. If we are not mindful, then lightness is a joke.

This is what my book *Meditation for Two*[105] is intended to demonstrate— the importance of starting with *being present*. When we are on the top of a horse and in a relaxed meditative state, then we can begin to figure out what is going on in our riding. Many people cannot be in this desired state of mind and body because they are not self-disciplined. When we are self-disciplined, meaning we can sit in the saddle and be *there* consciously, focusing on our breathing, then suddenly all the simple images of horse and man as one are very much part of our life...very much evident.

But people are decidedly *not* in the present. This is what their problem is—not the images they can or cannot visualize, not their riding, not their relationship with the horse, not all that—*it's their own state of mind*. Once again, *it is not what we do, it is what we are*. We must learn less to *do* and more to *be*. We must change our level of consciousness. And we do this through practice, practice, practice.

It is not what we do,
it is what we are.

the alchemy of lightness

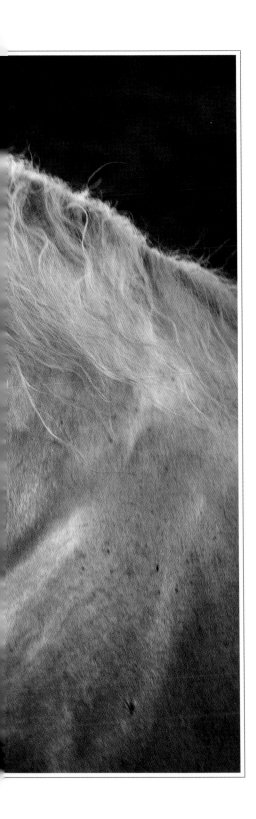

how observation is an important element in facilitating *molecular change*

When we have achieved the quality of consciousness just described, then we can *observe*. First, we need to be present; we need to find a different level of consciousness. This puts us in a place where we are *so aware* of everything with every fiber of our being that *observation is what we are*. We *are* the observation, we *see* the observation...we are part of the world that exists *in* that level of consciousness.

Therefore, the quality of our observation is really the quality of how present we are. Can we *stay in the moment* so we can *observe what we are doing* and at the same time *be part of it*?

Observation is part of creation. When we achieve the level of consciousness where *molecular change* is a possibility, we not only observe what is happening on the physical level, but we are also aware of the multitude of energies that surround us, and the difference between those energies, and how we can marry them together. For example, when we can see the energy of the rider, of the trainer, and of the horse, we can find ways to match them in order for them to vibrate together.

Practice the skill of observation. Repeatedly observe the same person and during intermolecular energy exchange, *you can become her or him instead of you*. Remember my story about training a horse to Grand Prix by *being* Mestre Oliveira (p. 78)? We can observe a person so deeply and completely that the experience *that* person has can also be ours at the same time, on whatever level we choose. And, if we are able to reproduce that experience on our own afterward, then it is part of us.

In Japan they used to say that we have to copy our master for 12 years before we can be proficient on our own. Modifying that replication is not necessary; we simply have to *copy our master*. *After* all those years of copying, *after* we have mimicked, *after* we have created *through* a different human being, *then* we can be the ones who create.

Perhaps 12 years can seem a little excessive, but it gives us an idea of how, on an everyday basis, we need to keep in the *same space* doing the *same things* on and beside our horse. Progressively, there is an essence of these things that become part of us, and *that* is when we become the creators.

the power of observation seen through a scientific lens

The simple act of observation can have an intense effect on how we ride and relate to our horses. Recent findings in quantum physics suggest reasons why our physical world can be changed by simply observing it.

The ancient book of Hindu verses known as "the Vedas" have demonstrated that *the act of observation and the means of observation cannot be separated from that which is being observed*.[106] Experiments[107-110] show that it is the act of our watching something, our *conscious observation*, that creates our *reality*. In other words, *the expectation or belief that we have while we're observing* is the ingredient in the soup that "chooses" what becomes real.[4]

To understand this we can draw on studies conducted earlier in the century that explore this concept on a molecular level. In a "quantum universe" where we all are interconnected, phenomena (what the senses or mind notice) and space and time are thought to be affected by the observer. All possibilities exist in the quantum "field"; the act of observation collapses them into probability. For example, the work of Alain Aspect (1982)[111] proved with physical science what mystics have long held true, that we are connected to all we observe by the very fact of our consciousness. In a similar experiment, Nobel Laureate Dr. John Wheeler[112, 113] sought to show that we are "connected to the stars" by the simple act of gazing at them.

The horse is a creature of unparalleled beauty, and what else would we rather observe than his grandeur? When motionless, when raising his body to the heavens, when solitary, and when one with a herd—the horse is deserving of our gaze. It is in that devoted observation that we begin to create our relationship of lightness.

clarity of intention

When we are clear in our *intention*—when we target our thoughts in an attempt to change physical reality through our determination to act in or be a certain way—*trust* is much easier to generate, particularly when another living being is involved. It shows up naturally. Trust is its own energetic bond. It is the exchange of energy between rider and horse that must be without barrier, and by necessity, without force, compression, or contraction. Generation of trust is the creation of the "bubble" that I spoke of earlier in this book (see p. 33). With some horses this process is easier than it is with others, to be sure, but our *intention* must always be *clear* in order for trust to come forth.

The horse is a creature of unparalleled beauty—what else would we rather observe than his grandeur?

clarity of intention seen through a scientific lens

Apollo 14 Astronaut Edgar Mitchell, founder of the Institute of the Noetic Sciences,[21] stated, "Trust the process. True intention is not so much a striving and a forcing...it is a letting go. It's an acknowledgement of allowing things in."[7] Numerous studies have documented the *power of intention*—even the phenomenon of *intentionality* at a distance has been explored by applying valid scientific standards.[114, 115] It is therefore possible, for example, to influence our horse's trot from a distance, in our longe work. And great horsemen know that, as teachers, they can assist students by creating the correct riding experience from a distance, through intention.

Human intention has been shown to be so powerful as to be able to change our body on a cellular level! Researchers were interested in the effects that intention produced on the DNA molecule,[116] and what they found defies our conventional understanding of our body. We have been conditioned to believe that the state of the DNA in our body is a given, that it's a fixed quantity—we "get what we get" when we're born—and with the exception of drugs, chemicals, and electrical fields, our DNA doesn't change in response to other input that naturally occurs over the course of our life. Results shared in a paper entitled *Effect of Conscious Intention on Human DNA* and presented at the International Forum on New Science in Denver, Colorado, in 1996 show us that nothing could be further from the truth.[117]

The power of intention was also studied by a team of scientists led by Japanese researcher and bestselling author Masaru Emoto. The goal of the study was to examine the effects of distant intention on water crystal formation. The experiment involved 1,900 participants from various locations in the world who focused their intention on water samples centrally located in California. This sophisticated study design was able to demonstrate an *actual change* in the "aesthetic rating" of the ice crystals that formed: The "intentionally treated" crystals were rated more beautiful than the control comparison group's crystals.[118]

Our *intention* has the power to affect the structure of water...even from a distance.[119] So how can we doubt its ability to change our relationship with our horse?

the happiness factor

I think *joy* is the most important ingredient in everything we do, say, share, and experience in this world. We see so many people who are *so serious* about things all the time. And, it's like the seriousness, the worry, the guilt—all that "fear stuff"—is killing the very essence of what they want to accomplish.

Joy is a product of *love,* which is one of the two emotions I've described in these pages as having a direct impact on our riding (see p. 35). Joy and love are thus, in effect, the same. When we are *happy* and able to *give happiness* to another, transmitting our joy and love to our horse and to other people, we experience what has to be one of the most powerful feelings known to man.

Constant perseverance means that we need to be dedicated to joy and the "giving" of happiness to others. We need to make an effort, a constant effort. It is so easy to get up in the morning and find 500 good reasons *not* be happy. We have only one real reason to be happy and that is that we *want* to be happy. Therefore, we need to "practice happiness." We need to "practice joy." And we need to *constantly remind ourselves to constantly be* in that state of joy.

There is always, in life, a serious situation. There are some moments when we must see the "true face of life," and sometimes it is not very enjoyable. But, I think that at the end of the day, we have to count our happy moments. (Our horse will love us for it!)

We have to make a decision about the "Happiness Factor" before our day starts: Are we going to the "Depressing World" or the "Happy World"? There are a lot of happy things, joyful things happening all around us. Just the simple act of putting a smile on our face produces many smiles in the people we meet each day. A smile goes a long way.

Remember, our mind can be our best friend or our worst enemy. We need to free ourselves from confirmed ego and from destructive emotions. This is the best thing we can do for ourselves and others. This is the best thing we can do for our horse.

the happiness factor seen through a scientific lens

In earlier chapters we introduced studies that illustrate how physical elements, such as our heart rhythm (heart rate pattern) and corresponding emotions, affect the horse, and how we are also, consequently, affected by the horse's physicality (the electromagnetic energy that emanates from the horse's heart, for example—see p. 54).

So, where do we start? Start with a smile! A "happier look"—even one artificially induced—has been shown to produce a "happier experience." Cosmetic surgeons recently found that removing "worry wrinkles" seemed to remove the underlying worry as well. This effect was stumbled upon when giving patients cosmetic injections of Botox—a protein present in botulism toxin used therapeutically to smooth facial lines. Cosmetic surgeons noticed that in Botox patients who were depressed, in some instances, the depression lifted after the injection.[121] *Changing the physical state had an impact on the mental state.* While we know that changing the mind changes the body, it also seems that the reverse is possible.

Changing our "mind" also induces physical changes in our brain. Through the use of functional magnetic resonance imaging (fMRI) and functional magnetic resonance spectroscopy (fMRS), which measure physiological parameters of brain activation, researchers have been able to document the changes occurring in the brain in conjunction with different emotional states. It is a sustained *state of appreciation* (demonstrated by increased blood flow to parts of the brain) that correlates with an identifiable physiological pattern linked to positive health outcomes and improved mental function.[62, 123] This physiological profile has also been shown to be associated with self-reports of "spiritual connectedness"[124] (a sense of purpose and meaning). Our horses are likely to feel this state and benefit from our commitment to cultivating and maintaining feelings of positive emotion.

Our horses benefit from our commitment to cultivating and maintaining feelings of positive emotion.

positive emotions affect
global consciousness

The idea that our emotions and our intention reach outward to affect the "global consciousness"—that when groups of people focus their minds on the same thing they influence "the world at large"—is currently being studied. For example, the Institute of Noetic Sciences has initiated the Noosphere Project and the Transformation Project, two global databases surveying thousands of individuals on the positive transformations of consciousness and creation of a "social consciousness"[125] —that is, social awareness and acknowledgment of the problems that different societies and communities face on a day-to-day basis, and a desire to explore alternatives to the dominant cultural viewpoint.

Why is this important to our connection with our horses? The hypothesis of the Global Coherence Initiative—a science-based, co-creative project to unite people in heart-focused care and intention—suggests that when a large number of people *intentionally generate positive emotions* the act elicits a "heart-coherent state" (see our earlier discussion of heart coherence on p. 32) that may be powerful enough to impact the earth's energetic and geomagnetic fields, perhaps even creating a kind of "global coherence"[126] (a world that is logical, orderly, aesthetically balanced).

So in the *really* big picture, our happiness, our relationship with ourselves, and the way we share our positive state of being with our horses has the capacity to not only transform us, but to transform the world.[127, 128]

keys to meeting the challenges
of the horse

Horses have the potential to give us the feelings of calm, peace, and love that we both crave and need. But horses are like children—they test us just to know if we have done our homework. Therefore, in order to be successful with them, we are required to be calm and compassionate— we must be calm and peaceful as we seek calm and peace; we must be loving in our search for love. This is an exercise in refinement. As we are ever more calm and peaceful, we will find our horse meeting us in that calm and peaceful place. It is an exchange that is unending.

When we begin work with our horse, we must be sure we are centered, *present* (see p. 99). We must tune out outside disturbances (physical or mental). We then need to tell our horse that we are working with him, for him, to make his life more joyful and to offer him a place to express himself fully. We need to believe that nothing can be wrong in our horse-manship and riding when our heart is in the right place.

Here are the keys to attaining and remaining in a higher state of consciousness with the horse, even when he challenges us:

1

Start with a plan but be ready to be flexible.

2

Identify and visualize a general idea of what you want.

3

Be prepared to ask firmly when necessary.

4

Know that you are and must be the leader of the dance.

5

Offer the horse a physical position that is without negative consequences.

6

Be ready to say, "No," without emotion.

7

Stay calm and "give" calmness to your horse when faced with disorder or excitement.

There is an order to the alchemy
of lightness. One thing cannot
come before another. One thing
cannot exist without the other.

the mind and biomechanics

When we add our mind to the biomechanics of the horse, we get the beginnings of the molecular process we have explored throughout these pages.

Let's say you have a horse—a young horse for example—that is working in hand. As you perform a movement, you think that the crossing of the front and hind legs is happening correctly (you can control the direction), but, you have the feeling that the horse is drifting to the outside. In other words, you lose the horse physically; therefore, you have lost him mentally.

In this example we can see how it is actually *you* who creates the problem. When you lose the horse "physically" by causing him to fall on the inside shoulder or to the outside, the horse does not fall, it is you who does not give the correct direction. The horse drifts (physically) when you are not focused (mentally) on the circle you wish to create. To remedy this problem perhaps you pull on the inside rein, but since you do not know where you are going you are unbalancing the horse. *It is a pilot error, not a horse error.*

In this situation, *you* must improve *your* mind, *your* focus, *your* direction, and then, progressively, the horse understands that *his* mind and body and *your* mind and body are together. After two or three days there is a chance for a *molecular change* as the horse becomes physically and mentally *with you*. And this change will be reflected in the biomechanics of the horse's movement when you next attempt work in hand.

common pitfalls that disrupt oneness with the horse

Most often, as I've mentioned time and again, people are *doing* and not *being*. People are not *present*—instead they are pulling on the reins; they are not looking where they are going; they do not have a clear understanding of what they want; they have no vision; they are leaning forward; their legs are banging against the horse; in general, they are totally stiff and rigid on the horse, and basically, they are not mentally "there."

Not being *present* is the worse offense. It is why when the horse loses focus or is startled, riders are so often caught by surprise. The keys to *being* and *staying present* are two elements from the Molecular Mantra we studied earlier: *Direction* (knowing and looking where you are going) and *Rhythm* (concentrating on the horse's energy and the pulse with which it transfers into movement). Additionally, we *must not* be pulling on the horse. Until these three things happen, none of the other building blocks can fall into place (see p. 16 for a complete description of the Molecular Mantra).

By progressively doing less and less while in the saddle, we eventually stay in that state—where we don't pull; where we look where we are going; where we concentrate on the energy from both our body and the horse's body. It is at this point that we can look for lightness. There is an order to the alchemy of lightness. One thing cannot come before another. One thing cannot exist without the other.

enhancing the relationship with the horse

The more self-disciplined we can become in our horsemanship, the better. Gaining awareness of our own body and mind is a sort of "general" fitness that allows us to become a part of our horse when working with him, both in and out of the saddle.

As the relationship with our body and mind—and our horse's—develops, we experience a different level of consciousness, one that is more elevated, where we are in a state of peace, safety, love, and happiness. The more elevated our consciousness, the more in tune our riding is going to be. Riding is not that much different from anything else in our life. When we are more and more conscious of shared energy, more and more giving of ourselves, and more and more compassionate, then our happiness will be proportional. This is very Zen thinking—the more you give, the happier you become. And happiness is not having things, it is giving things.

Most of the time our acts are in complete contradiction to our desires. We want happiness but we act toward trouble.

Check-In

Use these prompts to review the ideas we've discussed so far:

1

*How do we begin changing our level of consciousness,
and why is this important for our horse?*

2

*Describe how our consciousness has the power to
affect other living beings around us.*

3

*How does observation, clarity of intent, and
cultivation of happiness affect our riding and
enhance the intermolecular energy exchange
with our horse?*

4

*Identify issues that potentially interfere with the
intermolecular energy exchange between human
and horse.*

Living in Lightness

improving our relationship with our equine partner

Most people desire to "be happy" and many also want to "give" happiness to other people. But somehow, there is an error in translation when they swing into the saddle. They get up there and there are all these rules and regulations and expectations, and all that stuff really works against the final desired product— which is happiness for both rider and horse.

For example, let's say you are not living in the present moment, but you do hold the expectation that your horse will be better today than he was yesterday. Now that is a nice thought, but when it comes down to it, it's just a nice thought. If it becomes all that you want and you are set in that idea—it has to be that way—if it does not happen, you are miserable. Then you are unhappy with your horse, with yourself, with your family, with the world.

It turns out that *we are not in control of it all*. We are only in control of our smile and what we can change within ourselves. What "the rest of it" (the normal events and machinations of day-to-day existence) comes down to is that there isn't "good" or "bad," just what it is that day. When we *stay present* and accept and understand this very basic principle, then life is much easier.

When we are not "in the now" we either cannot have a relationship with our horse at all, or the relationship we have is a *terrible* one. Being with our horse, working with him, and riding him is more difficult than it should be. Suddenly, we feel we have to use force. This is usually because we have not helped the horse carry himself in the basic position necessary for understanding our aids and performing the movements, but since we are not *present*, it is not likely we realize that. Our body and mind are foreign to us and to the horse. And when we see this, we often see hardness, violence, and misunderstanding, as well.

In contrast, when we are fully alive and aware in the present moment, and when our heart is in the right place, then a certain *softness* is apparent. If we *meditate* and *contemplate* we acquire a very strong version of *kindness* that is necessary for there to be *softness*. This softness should *not* be confused with weakness. Some people are sweet and nice but weak—they do not possess the type of strength inherent in true kindness. There is a lot of power in kindness.

"staying present" seen through a scientific lens

The benefits of "staying present"—being self-aware up to the very moment—can be found in numerous studies and supported by vast amounts of documented anecdotal information. For example, in the book edited by scientist Francisco Varela, *Sleeping, Dreaming and Dying: An Exploration of Consciousness with the Dalai Lama,* we read how Tibetan monks achieve

When we are fully alive and aware in the present moment, and when our heart is in the right place, then a certain softness is apparent.

harmony with the "field of consciousness" and then possess the ability to perform mental and physical feats of strength and clarity that might otherwise be considered paranormal. As simplistic as the instructions to "stay in the present" might seem, the meditative practices involved influence the body in a very specific and compelling way, eliciting powerful reflexes that we can harness.[43] To ride with a physical prowess and subtlety and to visualize oneness with our horse with extreme clarity is ours to be had, if we can learn to "stay in the now"—let the past slip away and be not concerned about the future, but simply utterly absorbed in the moment.

chapter 6 — living in lightness

understanding that "being" is enough

Being present is one of the most difficult things there is to achieve. It requires self-discipline and meditative practice. Ideally, we must learn to sit happily on a meditation pillow and clear our mind and set aside all distractions before we try to sit happily on a horse. When we *are*—meaning when we are *present* and *mindful*—then suddenly our consciousness evolves and the *molecular change* we crave occurs. Whether we are doing *something* or doing *nothing*, we need to concentrate and be *100 percent aware of doing what we are doing—or not doing.* (I recommend studying the many works of Thích Nhât Hanh, a Buddhist monk, teacher, author, poet, and peace activist who has published more than 100 books.)

It is difficult to stay *present* when our mind is not disciplined: our emotions are everywhere, our thoughts are everywhere. We are constantly bombarded by energy and events and exterior "noise." And in some truth we *want* to be bombarded, because it is an excuse *not to stay present.* You see, sometimes it is very painful to stay "in the moment" because it is about serious and deep self-examination.

For example, recently I was speaking with my mother and told her, "Mother, I am working on my tolerance right now."

She said, with some surprise, "What?" and I replied, "I feel like I am very intolerant."

"Did somebody tell you that?" she asked.

"No mom, nobody told me," I admitted. "It's just that I sense it. I've looked long and hard at myself, and I see it."

When we are with the horse, we must be just as mindful as we are with ourselves. To *be* with the horse is just as challenging as it is to *be* in our everyday interactions with ourselves and others. To *be* in riding is to look where we are going, to know exactly the rhythm we want, to have a relationship with the physicality of our horse, and then to be open to something bigger than we are.

This program is a *life program*...a life's work. To *be present* is one thing but to *stay present* is another. We want to remain in the state of *being* as long as we can. This is very challenging and very demanding. It is basically the act of seeking enlightenment. We must look at ourselves that deeply.

finding "childlike innocence" and how it affects our relationship with the horse

Many great masters, like the Dalai Lama, have been deemed "childlike." How does this translate to our relationship with the horse?

It is not realistic to think that we will recover the same innocence we possessed as children. However, we can work to remember what it was like when we were children and attempt to again touch base with that "place." When we were children we were very *present* with few things to worry about—it was all about the "here and now," we had direction, we had ways to focus our energy. That stuff is inherent to childhood.

What is important to our horsemanship is that we remember those childlike qualities, because as we move through life, we tend to trend away from these characteristics of innocence. The good news is we do not actually lose them; we just forget them in the face of "more important matters." When we become mindful, though, we are reminded of what is important in life. Generally we return to state of the child—the state of humor, of curiosity, of happiness. We can remember how beautiful life can be to a child with that sort of simplicity of feeling.

Horses are not intellectual beings. We need to be in this simpler, more innocent, childlike space with them, a place so clear and so beautiful that just being there with them offers us purity.

how our relationship with our horse affects our soul

When we purposely let ourselves become "disconnected from the joy" that surrounds us and that is ours for the taking, when we do not allow joy to be our guide, then I believe our soul is not "happy." I have this rather childlike image of a "soul" in my mind's eye, and this sense that our soul is only happy when *everyone* is happy.

The connection that we have with nature, with animals in general and with horses in particular, is such a *source* of joy. To actually feel we can *be one* with another being confirms that we are a part of creation, a part of every single thing that happens. When we disconnect from the present moment—and therefore from nature, animals, horses, creation—then we are basically miserable...joyless. I see people all around us disconnecting from the world, looking at it from a very hard angle—from an "ego standpoint," consisting of a limited view centered around individual identity. They blame their profession for it; they blame their education or their religion. Whatever the cause, the fact of the matter is that their disconnection binds them to an exclusivity of self that creates *separateness*, rather than *togetherness*. We cannot be one with the horse when we are totally absorbed in our individual self.

We need to be in a simple, more innocent, "childlike" space with our horses—a place so clear and so beautiful that just being there with them offers us purity.

the alchemy of lightness

When we make an effort to *reconnect*, to sit close to our horse, to be with him, breathe with him, and feel that oneness, that togetherness, then we reconnect with something that is so fundamentally part of us that when we look at it again, we see it *is* us.

The act of "creating" with our horse expands our consciousness and allows us to express love and brilliance in a dynamic way—a way that we may not have discovered in any other practice of endeavor.

When we ride a horse, we either *reinforce* or *rise above* our lack of connection. Review our discussion of grounding on p. 41. Remember, when we ride, we need to accept and trust the grounding of the horse. The horse amplifies our feelings, so if we feel disconnected before we mount, we will feel 100 times more disconnected in the saddle. If we feel good and connected, we will feel 100 times better on the horse's back.

When those who are disconnected allow themselves to reconnect, they will find that their horse is like a "secret weapon" that makes them feel bigger, stronger, and more empowered. The horse is a guidepost to help them get in touch with their true nature.

The thing about horses is that we do not even need to sit on them. Just the *Darshan*—the receipt of blessings from a guru—or in other words *just looking at them*, is enough for people to be touched deeply. Again, this is due to the molecular process that occurs. We are so overwhelmed by a feeling of togetherness with our horse that it takes over our whole body, our whole mind.

Molecular change happens all the time. While it is perhaps not within our power to enact the change itself, we *can* create the situations that allow the change to happen. It often happens suddenly. Many times we really do not know how it occurred. As we've discussed in this book, we can prepare ourselves for *molecular change*. We can sort of work on it in advance so when we have the situation where the change can happen, it does. We just wake up one morning and feel totally uplifted and happy and that heaviness of ego and disconnection has left us.

When working with our horse, we must not think of ourselves—we must think of our horse.

the alchemy of lightness

Sometimes we wake up and feel that this heaviness has come back. Sometimes we feel the tendencies of depression returning, chasing away the joy. We have to deal with these issues all the time and remain devoted to creating a physical, mental, and molecular environment that nurtures being *present*, being *connected*, and attaining a *higher level of consciousness* on and off the horse. *This* is what Molecular Equitation is all about.

Change is a creative act.

change is never bad

I am a firm believer that, in general, there are no bad changes. Change can be uncomfortable when it occurs, but when we have a change it is generally for the better. We need to be able to welcome change, to "put it out there" that we are ready for change anytime so we can learn something on a deeper level or for the betterment of ourselves or others. There is a lot of creativity that comes with this kind of attitude, this kind of openness. We are part of a creative process.

dealing with expectations

We live in a society that teaches that happiness comes from the *outside*. It is therefore difficult for many to conceptualize that happiness actually comes from *inside*—inside all of us.

Everyone wants a "good ride," whether on a horse or through life, but we set ourselves up to experience the contrary. We don't live in the present moment. We build from the problems of past experiences onto our future need: "I need to be Third Level this year," or "I need to get my medal this year." The horse is never consulted about our new agenda, our new expectations—the show at which we want to compete or the award we want to win. Our riding partner is ignorant of expectations.

When we find ourselves in difficult situations while riding or working with our horse, we must not think of ourselves. We must think about our horse, asking ourselves: Is he okay? Is he having difficulty moving a certain way? How can I help him? When we change the focus to our horse, we will see our own frustration go away instantly.

We put a lot of effort into improving the outside condition of our life, but in the end, it is always our mind that experiences the world as bringing joy or causing suffering. Therefore, *if we transform our way of perceiving things, we can transform the quality of our life,* as stated by Matthew Ricard, the personal translator of the Dalai Lama.

As we've explored throughout these pages, we need to allow for a new state of consciousness so we can see things differently. We need to train our mind to calm down and learn to just *be*. For, it is when *we change* that the horse has a chance to be himself. It is with *our change* that the world will change. It is with *our change* that there springs forth a new chance for better health and understanding the world over.

learning to embrace change

Learning means being open to change. We need to learn to live with passion and curiosity. In life, in general, especially with horses, our relationships tend to be hesitant and incomplete. We *sort of* know what we want but are unsure of how to communicate it.

How can we learn to embrace change and "complete" our relationship with our horse so we are no longer separate beings but instead *one*?

1

Nurture clarity of feeling—that primordial, "childlike innocence" we discussed on p. 119.

2

Find a common pursuit that both you and your horse can enjoy.

3

Change your mind about how difficult everything in the saddle can be. A common misconception about riding is that it is very complicated and mastered only by knowing complicated theories. Instead, try to keep it very simple. Another is that it is difficult for horse and rider to find balance together, and this becomes a constant obstacle, even though it does not exist most of the time. Largely, it is ignorance regarding basic tools of communication and the use of inefficient and rude aids that are the problem. Another false belief is that fine riding is not within everyone's reach and reserved for a few select individuals. I consider all these false and completely unnecessary obstacles.

limiting our limitations

My riding master used to say, *there is the art and there is the mind*. In other words, there is the *art* of riding, and there is the *technique* of riding. Yes, we need to know enough technique that the physical does not work against us: We need to have some knowledge about how our body works and how to control it (body awareness). We need to have some understanding of the horse and his ways, and a grasp on the biomechanics of his movement. We need enough technique to create the physical space where we can join with the horse and *be one*...and that's it.

Some riders "kill," by rudeness and force, the possibility of the creation of the artistic dimension. Do not let the study and application of technique limit artistic creation. We need technique to allow the horse to express himself—for example, we must be able to put the horse on the bit (see p. 58)—but thinking only of technique will prohibit oneness.

When we have achieved
Openness and Release, we have
found Lightness.

A horse might have perfect conformation, but when his heart is not in it, he is not an ideal dressage horse because he does not like what he is doing. A horse with less perfect conformation but with "heart" does much better. It is the same with riders. The more athletic the horse, the more athletic the rider, perhaps the better the partnership—but it is not always true. It has more to do with our heart's capacity as a catalyst; the willingness of the rider and horse to create *molecular change* and meld as one.

There is the art of riding, and there is the technique of riding.

the brown bag

I learned, from my friend and astrologer Steven Forrest, that life goes into cycles of roughly 30-year periods. Every 30 years, we experience a full turn of all the planets. So, in the first 30 years we are trying to figure things out; in the second 30 years we try to do what we figured out; and in the last 30 years, we reassess a few things we did.

As we might do during the last 30-year period described by Steven Forrest, at times we must reassess our life. We must look at things that bothered us: our relationship with a partner; our business not going the way it should be; our dog behaving poorly...whatever it might be and however seemingly minor.

Imagine taking all those things that bother you about life up until this moment and putting them into a brown paper bag. Picture yourself closing the bag, rolling down the top very tightly, then going to a bridge over a fast-flowing river and very politely dropping your bag over the side and into the rushing water below. Imagine leaning over the side of the bridge and watching your brown paper bag float away.

The point of this exercise is that when we identify all the things we do not like or that we want to change and then "release" them—let them go— then we create space and energy to allow change to happen. (Remember, I think change is almost always a good thing—see p. 123.) We have to let go of what we may have wanted or what we once thought we should be... we have to let go of all our expectations. When we *release* the brown bag, we will discover that our partner, our horse, the universe, will open to us.

Openness and Release are the final building block in the "Molecular Mantra" I introduced at the beginning of this book (see p. 16). Their molecular "parallel" is *Lightness*. Therefore, when we have achieved *Openness and Release*, we have found *Lightness*.

rejoicing in abundance

Not so long ago, I was in Chicago for a clinic around Father's Day, and I received a package containing a beautiful new shirt. It was sent from Barbier Farm, my place, with a personal note from my wife and letters from my two children (which I did not think they knew how to write!), telling me what a wonderful father I was. A simple gesture, maybe, but it was one that had never happened in my life before, and I was very touched. I immediately picked up the phone and thanked them...I had to wait 60 years to have this wonderful surprise package "happen," and I felt very blessed.

And then, a few months later I came home one day and my wife Debra said, "By the way...we are going fishing next month. I organized a trip. It's all set." This again might not seem like much, but in my private life I had always organized vacations and holidays. This was the first time that Debra had done so.

I could go on and on listing more examples of sudden changes that occurred as I began my last 30-year period, but the point is that when I reassessed and put all the things I did not like or that I wanted to change in a "brown paper bag" and released them, I created the space and energy for the other people in my life to open to me. Suddenly, the giving was all around. Suddenly, there was *abundance*.

Final Check-In

Use these prompts to review the ideas we've discussed so far:

1

*What are the consequences when we fail to
be "present" with our horse?*

2

*How is being "childlike" important to
good horsemanship?*

3

*Consider the ways we can learn to welcome change
in our life and in our riding.*

4

*Fill an imaginary "brown paper bag" with all the things
in your life and in your horsemanship that you are not
happy with, picture yourself leaning over the side of a
bridge, drop that full bag down into the flowing river
below…and watch it float away.*

An End and a Beginning

Developing a loving partnership with our horse, one that allows for "co-creation"—combining and renewing our own abilities with those of our horse in an effort to discover and share brilliance and light—begins with our *intention*. Intention demands that we examine our life, our motives, and our way of being. My friend, the photographer Keron Psillas, has a saying: "We photograph as we are." Well, we *ride as we are*...we *live our life as we are*. Becoming aware of *who we are* is an ongoing process of refinement, like peeling away the layers of an onion. And everything we touch in the course of our life reflects that process—which layer is exposed at any given time.

In my own life, each time I have thought I have uncovered something new about myself—about my consciousness—I have been excited to share it with my horses. But I have always discovered that they are already "there." They are not only helping us to achieve our highest transformation, they are waiting for us when we arrive at each stop on the journey, when we negotiate each turn on the path.

Going forward, as you meditate on your relationship with your horse, with others, with yourself, remember your breathing and intent. When you go to the barn to see your horse, arrive with a smile. *Bring the joy with you* that your horse so often gives you so it will be amplified when you are together. We can call this amplified joy many things: a "heart connection," healing, transformation, togetherness. As we have discovered in these pages, it is *molecular change* that leads to a higher energy frequency, a "vibration of love" that enables us to achieve a greater sense of oneness with our horse.

You will discover that you can apply the messages of Molecular Equitation that I've shared in this book in all the areas of your life; in fact, it will be impossible *not to* change your life as you will have transformed yourself through your intention and the partnership of your horse. Honor the gift your horse is waiting to give you. Be present with him. Joy is waiting; beauty is waiting. It is there for all of us to experience.

Amities,
D. Barbier

a request to the reader

I write this ending with a request to the reader that he or she revisit the photo selected as the cover of this book. This image, taken by Keron Psillas in Brazil, has been the piece that has always fascinated me. This image is the essence of why I took on this project.

I came to this book, not as a scientist, but as a horsewoman with a scientific backdrop. My quest was to further understand and help explain what I know happens when horse and human are one, and what Dominique's life's work has been about. My hope is that this text makes the possibility of this "magic" accessible to people. This book has been the culmination of nearly three years of collaboration. It represents hundreds of hours of my having transcribed discussions, organized relevant science, and generated ideas and questions. Over the years of working with horses and their humans, I have been a sounding board for people's questions around how to facilitate this kind of connection with their horse. My hope is that here, these "heart" questions have been answered. Stay open, stay kind, stay connected.

Dr. Maria Katsamanis

Endnotes/References

My ability to record details of note that may pertain to the pursuit of lightness and equestrian art is limited to the pages prior; however, for those interested in the specifics of the studies cited, references follow in the form of endnotes so that further review can be had. It is my feeling that the texts included represent a novel way to understand the relationship we have with ourselves, with our horses, and with the greater cosmos.

1. Lipton BH. *The Biology of Belief*. California: Hay House; 2008.
2. Emoto M. *The Hidden Messages in Water*. New York: Atria Books; 2005.
3. Church D. *The Genie in Your Genes*. California: Elite Books; 2007.
4. Braden G. *The Divine Matrix*. California: Hay House, Inc.; 2007.
5. Hanna T. *The Body of Life: Creating New Pathways for Sensory Awareness and Fluid Movement*. Vermont: Healing Arts Press; 1993.
6. Kelly R. *The Human Antenna*. California: Energy Psychology Press; 2006.
7. McTaggart L. *The Field*. New York: HarperCollins Publishers; 2002.
8. McTaggart L. *The Intention Experiment*. New York: Free Press; 2007.
9. Peirce P. *Frequency: The Power of Personal Vibration*. New York: Simon & Schuster; 2009.
10. Pert CB. *Molecules of Emotion*. New York: Scribner; 1997.
11. Yurth DG. *Seeing Past the Edge*: Fifth Edition; 2007.
12. Radin DI, Taylor RD, Braud W. Remote mental influence of human electrodermal activity: A pilot replication. *European Journal of Parapsychology*. 1995;11:19.
13. The Institute of HeartMath was founded in 1991 as a nonprofit research organization "providing a range of unique services p, and technologies to boost performance, productivity, health and well-being while dramatically reducing stress." For more information, please visit the website: www.HeartMath.com/company/index.html.
14. Davidson RJ, Kabat-Zinn J. *Alterations in Brain and Immune Function Produced by Mindfulness Meditation: Three Caveats: Response*: Psychosomatic Medicine January/February 2004;66(1):149-152.
15. Gehrke EK. New Meaning to "Horse Sense". *A Change of Heart*. 2006;5(1):1.
16. Hanggi EB, Ingersoll JF. Stimulus discrimination by horses under scotopic conditions. *Behavioural Processes*. Sep 2009;82(1):45-50.
17. Hanggi EB. Equine Research Foundation. http://www.equineresearch.org/
18. Backster C. Biocommunication with plants, living foods, and human cells. *Primary Perception*. 2003.
19. McCraty Rea. Electrophysiological evidence of intuition: Part 2: A system-wide process? *Journal of Alternative & Complementary Medicine*. 2004;10(2):325.
20. Radin D, Nelson R, Dobyns Y, et al. Reexamining Psychokinesis: Comment on Bosch, Steinkamp, and Boller. [Editorial] *Psychological Bulletin*. 2006;132(4):529-532.

21. For a database of meditation studies stIoNSws, specifically http://noetic.org/research/medbiblio/index.htm (accessed January 3, 2007).

22. Dubrovsky V. Elastic Model of a Physical Vacuum (in Russian). *DAN USSR*. 1985;282(1).

23. Nimtz G. Superluminal Signal Velocity. *Annalen der Physik*. 1998;7(618).

24. Nimtz H. Superluminal Photonic Tunneling and Quantum Electonics. *Progress in Quantum Electronics*. 1997;21(81).

25. Enders A, H.W. N. Photonic Tunneling Experiments. *Physics Review*. 1993;B47(9605).

26. Enders A, Nimtz G. On Superluminal barrier Transversal. *Journal of Physics (France)*. 1992;2:1693.

27. Associated Press. Light Can Break Its Own Speed Limit; 2000.

28. Epigenetics special issue. *Science*. 2001;293:5532.

29. Braden G. *The God Code*: Hay House; 2005.

30. Pert C. The Mind/Body Connection.177-181.

31. Damasio Rea. Subcortical and cortical brain activity during the feeling of self-generated emotions. *Nature Neuroscience*. 2000;3:1049.

32. Lovelock J. *The Ages of Gaia*: WW Norton; 1995.

33. Capra F. *The Turning Point*: Bantam; 1984.

34. Kafatos, M. *The Conscious Universe*: Nadeau R. Springer; 1999.

35. Bose JC, ed. *Live Movements in Plants, Transactions of the Bose Research Institute*. New York: Outerbridge and Lazard, Inc; 1972. C. Muses AMY, ed. Consciousness and Reality: The Human Pivot.

36. Tompkins P, Bird C. *The Secret Life of Plants*: Avon Books; 1973.

37. Hashimoto. Dr. Hashimoto's books were printed in Japan in Japanese and are currently out of print. However, copies can be acquired by contacting http://www.iuniverse.com/. *Additional information can be obtained from the Library of Congress, either by direct correspondence or online.*

38. Nelson JH. *The Propagation Wizard's Handbook: Coping With Our Occult Sun and its Meddlesome Satellites*; 1978.

39. Volland. op.cit. for extensive references and annotated bibliography.

40. Schnabel J, (1997). *Remote Viewers: The Secret History of America's Psychic Spies*. New York: Dell.

41. Gorightly A. The Journal of Possible Paradigms: found at http://www.elfis.net/elfol4/e4pkdomc.html.

42. Volland. op.cit., Schumann Resonance follow-up studies, references.

43. Laszlo E. *The Whispering Pond: A Personal Guide to the Emerging Vision of Science*; 1996.

44. Monroe, R. The Monroe Institute.

45. Morris S. Heart-Focused Breathing: A good way to get started on the path to increasing your energy, coherence and resilience. *Institute of HeartMath Newsletter*. 2010;9(4).

46. Goswami A. The Scientific Evidence for God Is Already Here. *Light of Consciousness*. 2004;16(3):32.

47. Ellison K. Secrets of the Buddha mind. *Psychology Today*. 2006:74.

48. Lehrer P, Vaschillo E, Lu S-E, et al. Heart rate variability biofeedback: effects of age on heart rate variability, baroreflex gain, and asthma. *Chest*. Feb 2006;129(2):278-284.

49. Lehrer PM, Woolfolk RL, Rooney AJ, McCann B, Carrington P. Progressive relaxation and meditation. A study of psychophysiological and therapeutic differences between two techniques. *Behaviour Research & Therapy*. 1983;21(6):651-662.

50. Sargunaraj D, Lehrer PM, Hochron SM, Rausch L, Edelberg R, Porges SW. Cardiac rhythm effects of .125-Hz paced breathing through a resistive load: implications for paced breathing therapy and the polyvagal theory. *Biofeedback & Self Regulation*. Jun 1996;21(2):131-147.

51. Song HS, Lehrer PM. The effects of specific respiratory rates on heart rate and heart rate variability. *Applied Psychophysiology & Biofeedback*. Mar 2003;28(1):13-23.

52. Giardino ND, Lehrer PM, Feldman JME. The role of oscillations in self-regulation: Their contributions to homeostasis: Harwood Publishing Company; 2000.

53. Lehrer, SM H, Mayne T, et al. Relationship between changes in EMG and respiratory sinus arrhythmia in a study of relaxation therapy for asthma. *Applied Psychophysiology & Biofeedback*. Sep 1997;22(3):183-191.

54. Lehrer, Vaschillo, Vaschillo. Resonant frequency biofeedback training to increase cardiac variability: rationale and manual for training. *Applied Psychophysiology & Biofeedback*. Sep 2000;25(3):177-191.

55. Lehrer P & Vaschillo E. Heart rate variability biofeedback: A new tool for improving autonomic homeostasis and treating emotional and psychosomatic diseases. *Japanese Journal of Biofeedback*. 2004;30:7-16.

56. Spicuzza L, Gabutti A, Porta C, Montano N, Bernardi L. Yoga and chemoreflex response to hypoxia and hypercapnia.[see comment][erratum appears in Lancet 2000 Nov 4;356(9241):1612]. *Lancet*. Oct 28 2000;356(9240):1495-1496.

57. Bernardi L, Sleight P, Bandinelli G, et al. Effect of rosary prayer and yoga mantras on autonomic cardiovascular rhythms: comparative study. *BMJ*. Dec 22-29 2001;323(7327):1446-1449.

58. McCraty ea. Electrophysiological evidence of intuition: Part I. The surprising role of the heart. *Journal of Alternative & Complementary Medicine*. 2004;10(1):133.

59. Radin D, Borges A. Intuition through time: what does the seer see? *Explore*. 2009;5(4): 200-211.

60. Radin DI. Electrodermal Presentiments of Future Emotions. *Journal of Scientific Exploration*. 2004;18(2):253-273.

61. McCraty R. The Energetic Heart: Bioelectromagnetic Communication Within and Between People. *Clinical Applications of Bioelectromagnetic Medicine*. New York: P. J. Rosch and M. S. Markov; 2004:541-562.

62. McCraty R, Atkinson M, Tiller W. The Role of Physiological Coherence in the Detection and Measurement of Cardiac Energy Exchange Between People. Paper presented at: Proceedings of the Tenth International Montreux Congress on Stress, 1999; Montreux, Switzerland.

63. McCraty R, Atkinson M, Tomasino D, Tiller W. The Electricity of Touch: Detection and Measurement of Cardiac Energy Exchange Between People. *Brain and Values: Is a Biological Science of Values Possible*. Mahwah, NJ: Lawrence Erlbaum Associates: Karl H. Pribram; 1998:359-379.

64. Radin D. Event-Related Electroencephalographic Correlations Between Isolated Human Subjects. *The Journal of Alternative and Complementary Medicine*. 2004;10(2):315-323.

65. Schlitz M, Wiseman R, Watt C, Radin D. Of two minds: Sceptic-proponent collaboration within parapsychology. *The British Psychological Society*. 2006;97:313-322.

66. Radin D, Schlitz M. Gut feelings, intuition, and emotions: An exploratory study. *The Journal of Alternative and Complementary Medicine*. 2005;11(1):85-91.

67. Bekoff M, Balcombe J. Minds of Their Own: Exploring the emotional and moral lives of animals. *AllAnimals*. 2010:32-35.

68. Hanggi EB. The thinking horse: cognition and perception reviewed. Paper presented at: Proceedings of the 51st American Association of Equine Practitioners Annual Convention, 2005; Seattle, WA.

69. Heuschmann G. *Tug of War: Classical Versus Modern Dressage: Why Classical Training Works and How Incorrect Riding Negatively Affects Horses' Health* Trafalgar Square Books 2007.

70. Bradley RT. The psychophysiology of entrepreneurial intuition: A quantum-holographic theory. Paper presented at: In Proceedings of the Third AGSE International Entrepreneurship Research Exchange, 2006; Auckland, New Zealand.

71. Tomasino D. The Psychophysiological Basis of Creativity and Intuition: Accessing "The Zone" of Entrepreneurship. *International Journal of Entrepreneurship and Small Business.* 2007:1-9.

72. Clark DO. From Philosopher to Psychologist: The Early Career of Edwin Ray Guthrie, Jr. *History of Psychology.* 2005;8:235-254.

73. Hanggi EB, Ingersoll JF. Long-term memory for categories and concepts in horses (Equus caballus). *Animal Cognition.* May 2009;12(3):451-462.

74. Hanggi EB. Equine cognition and perception: Understanding the horse. In: Itakura FS, ed. *Diversity of Cognition.* Japan; 2006:86-118.

75. Hanggi EB. Can horses recognize pictures? . Paper presented at: Proceedings of the Third International Conference of Cognitive Science, 2001; Beijing, China.

76. Norretranders T. *The User Illusion.* New York: Viking Penguin; 1998.

77. Merriam Webster's dictionary definition of consciousness.

78. Weil A. *Dr. Andrew Weil's Self-Healing*; 2006.

79. Keeling L. Investigating horse-human interactions: the effect of a nervous human, *The Veterinary Journal* 2009.

80. Myers DG. *Theories of Emotion Psychology: Seventh Edition.* New York, NY: Worth Publishers; 2004.

81. Rein G, Atkinson M, McCraty R. The Physiological and Psychological Effects of Compassion and Anger *Journal of Advancement in Medicine.* 1995;8(2):87-103.

82. Motz J. Everyone as Energy Healer: The Treat V Conference. Paper presented at: Advances: The Journal of Mind-Body Health, 1993; Santa Fe, NM.

83. Rein G, McCraty R. Structural Changes in Water and DNA Associated with New Physiologically Measureable States. *Journal of Scientific Exploration.* 1994;8(3):438-439.

84. Backster C. *Primary Perception: Biocommunication with plants, living foods and human cells*: White Rose Millennium Press; 2003.

85. Gariaev PP, Grigor'ev AA, Vasil'ev VP, Poponin, Shcheglov VA. Investigation of the Fluctuation Dynamics of DNA Solutions by Laser Correlation Spectroscopy. *Bulletin of the Lebedev Physics Institute.*

86. Poponin V. *"The DNA Phantom Effect: Direct Measurement of a New Field in the Vacuum Substructure," performed the Russian study again in 1995 under the auspices of the Institute of HeartMath, Research Division, Boulder Creek, CA* 1995.

87. Coetzee H. Biomagetism and bio-electromagnetism: the foundation of life. *Future History.* 2000;8.

88. Liboff AR. Toward an electromagnetism paradigm for biology and medicine. *Journal of Alternative & Complementary Medicine.* 2004;10(1):41.

89. Beneviste Jea. Highly dilute antigen increases coronary flow of isolated heart from immunized guinea-pigs. *FASEB Journal.* 1992;6:A1610.

90. Beneviste Jea. Transatlantic transfer of digitized antigen signal by telephone link. *Journal of Allergy & Clinical Immunology.* 1997;99:S175.

91. Grad B. Some biological effects of "laying on of hands". *Journal of the American Society for Psychical Research.* 1965;59:95.

92. Porges SW. The polyvagal perspective. *Biological Psychology.* Feb 2007;74(2):116-143.

93. Vaschillo E, Vaschillo B, Lehrer PM. Heartbeat synchronizes with respiration rhythm only under specific circumstances. *Chest.* 2004;126:1385-1386.

94. Lehrer PM, Vaschillo E, Vaschillo B, et al. Heart rate variability biofeedback increases baroreflex gain and peak expiratory flow. *Psychosomatic Medicine.* Sep-Oct 2003;65(5):796-805.

95. Lehrer P, Sasaki Y, Saito Y. Zazen and Cardiac Variability. *Psychosomatic Medicine.* 1999;61:812-821.

96. Bernardi L, Sleight P, Bandinelli G, et al. Effect of rosary prayer and yoga mantras on autonomic cardiovascular rhythms: comparative study. *British Medical Journal* 2001;323(7372):1446-1449.

97. Oikawa O, Malinovsky I, Kotay A, et al. Heart Rate Variability Biofeedback: New Directions in Collaborative Medical and Related Healthcare Research. *Japanese. Journal of Biofeedback Research*. 2007;34(2):17-21.

98. Karavidas MK, Lehrer PM, Vaschillo E, et al. Preliminary results of an open label study of heart rate variability biofeedback for the treatment of major depression. *Appl Psychophysiol Biofeedback*. Mar 2007;32(1):19-30.

99. Hassett AL, Radvanski DC, Vaschillo EG, et al. A Pilot Study of the Efficacy of Heart Rate Variability (HRV) Biofeedback in Patients with Fibromyalgia. *Appl Psychophysiol Biofeedback*. Mar 2007;32(1):1-10.

100. Ginsberg JP, Berry ME, Powell DA. Improving Cognition in Recently Returned Combat Veterans with Posttraumatic Stress Disorder by Heart Rate Variability Coherence Biofeedback. Columbia, SC: Shirley L. Buchanan Neuroscience Laboratory, Dorn VA Medical Center; 2010.

101. Gillin M, La Pira F, McCraty R, et al. Before Cognition: The Active Contribution of the Heart/ANS to Intuitive Decision Making as Measured on Repeat Entrepreneurs in the Cambridge Technopol. Paper presented at: Paper to be presented at the Fourth AGSE International Entrepreneurship Research Exchange, 2007; Brisbane, Australia.

102. Beck R. Mood modification with ELF magnetic fields: A preliminary exploration. *Archaeus*. 1986:4.

103. Trudeau M. Student's view of intelligence can help grades. *NPR Your Health.* 2007.

104. Bower B. Mind over muscle: placebo boosts health benefits of exercise. *Science News Online*. 2007;171(4).

105. Barbier D, Psillas K. *Meditation for Two*; 2010.

106. Doniger W. (editor) W, W., O'Flaherty, T..D (editor) . , ed. *The Rig Veda: An Anthology: One Hundred Eight Hymns, Selected, Translated and Annotated (classic)*: Viking Press; 1982.

107. From an interview with John Wheeler by Tim Folger, "Does the Universe Exist if We're Not Looking?". Vol 23: Discover:44.

108. Aspect A, Dalibard J, Roger G. Experimental Test of Bell's Inequalities Using Time-varying Analyzers. *Physical Review Letters*. 1982;49.

109. Schmidt M, Selleri F. Empty Wave Effects on Particle Trajectories in Triple-Slit Experiments. *Found. Phys. Lett.* 1991;4(1).

110. Radin D. Testing nonlocal observation as a source of intuitive knowledge. *The Journal of Science and Healing.* 2007.

111. Aspect A, Dalibard J, Roger G. Experimental Test of Bell's Inequalities Using Time-varying Analyzers. *Physical Review Letters* 1982;49(1804).

112. Wheeler JA. *Einstein's Vision*: Springer-Verlag; 1968.

113. Wheeler JA, Zurek WH. *Quantum Theory and Measurement*. Princeton, N.J.: Princeton University Press; 1983.

114. Schlitz M, Braud W. Distant Intentionality and healing: Assessing the evidence. *Alternative Therapies in Health and Medicine,*. 1997;3(6):62-73.

115. Dossey L. How healing happens: Exploring the nonlocal gap. *Alternative Therapies in Health and Medicine,*. 2002;8(2):103-110.

116. Rein G. *Effect of Conscious Intention on Human DNA.*

117. Rein G. Effect of Conscious Intention on Human DNA. Paper presented at: Proceedings of the International Forum on New Science, 1996; Denver, CO.

118. Radin D, Hayssen G, Emoto M, Kizu T. Double-Blind Test of the Effects of Distant Intention on Water Crystal Formation. *Explore*. 2006;2(5):408-411.

119. Tomasino D, 1997. *New Technology Provides Scientific Evidence of Water's Capacity to Store and Amplify Weak Electromagnetic and Subtle Energy Fields.* Boulder Creek, CA HeartMath Research Center.

120. Radin D, Taft R, Yount G. Effects of Healing Intention on Cultured Cells and Truly Random Events. *The Journal of Alternative and Complementary Medicine.* 2004;10(1): 103-112.

121. Botox lifts brows---and spirits. *Washington Post*, 2006.

122. Richards T, McCraty R, Atkinson M. Functional Magnetic Resonance Imaging and Spectroscopy of Brain Activation During Heart Rhythm Coherence. Paper presented at: Toward a Science of Consciousness Conference, 2002; Tuscon, Arizona.

123. McCraty R, Atkinson M, Tomasino D, Bradley RT. *The Coherent Heart: Heart–Brain Interactions, Psychophysiological Coherence, and the Emergence of System-Wide Order.* Boulder Creek, CA: HeartMath Research Center, Institute of HeartMath; 2006.

124. Childre D, McCraty R. Psychophysiological Correlates of Spiritual Experience. *Biofeedback.* 2001:13-17.

125. Schlitz M, Vieten C, Miller E. Worldview Transformation and the Development of Social Consciousness. *Journal of Consciousness Studies.* 2010;17(7-8):18-36.

126. McCraty R, Childre D. Coherence: Bridging Personal, Social, and Global Health. *Alternative Therapies in Health and Medicine.* 2010;16(4):10-24.

127. Nelson R, Bancel P, Radin D. *Global Consciousness Project: Noosphere Project*: The Institute of Noetic Sciences.

128. Schlitz M, Vieten C, Amorok T. *The Transformation Project*: The Institute of Noetic Sciences.

Acknowledgments

dominique barbier

To my dad who believed in my early day dedication. To old students and riders who share my passion in looking deeper into the horse and into themselves.

I would like to thank my wife Debra, who helped me develop the process. Also my co-author Maria Stamatiou Katsamanis, for finding the scientific background that I needed for this book. Her "researcher's mind" was a great help. Thank you to Keron Psillas, my longtime accomplice, for editorial assistance, great photographs, and a lot more. To Michael Charters for putting lots of thoughts together. And thank you to my editor Rebecca Didier and to Martha Cook and Caroline Robbins at Trafalgar Square Books, who made this publication possible.

maria katsamanis

Thank you to those who said that I could...and to those who said that I couldn't.

About the Authors and Photographer

dominique barbier

Dominique Barbier was born in France in 1950. In 1962, he began his equine career at a Jesuit school in Poitiers, France, and at 15, he attended Crabett Park School in England where he received his British Horse Society Assistant Instructor (BHSAI). In 1972, Dominique returned to England to attend the Talland School of Equitation in Cirenchester, where Mrs. Molly Siveright, FBHS, DBHS, instructed him. He continued riding throughout Europe at numerous facilities in various disciplines, including jumping, eventing, dressage, and steeplechase. Dominique then went to Portugal to study two years with Mestre Nuno Oliveira. Through his internship with Mestre Oliveira, Dominique learned to ride by perfecting his "mental and physical attitude." The experience became a turning point in his riding career and inspired his belief in keeping the horse light and happy: "la belle légèreté à la francaise." While in Portugal, Dominique purchased Dom Pasquale, Dom Giovanni, and Dom Jose, three Lusitano stallions that were to be the first he would train to high school levels. In addition, Dom Giovanni learned to canter on the spot and to canter backward.

Since immigrating to the United States, Dominique's teaching and passion for the "Art of Dressage" has reached many thousands of people around the world. Ahead of his time, Dominique has been teaching the importance of mental communication and the understanding of the horse's nature for nearly forty years. His critically acclaimed book, *Dressage for the New Age*, was revolutionary to the dressage world when first published, with its consideration of the horse's psychology and well-being as the cornerstones of training. *Dressage for the New Age*, now in its third edition in English, has also been published in French, Portuguese, and German. He is the author of a number of other books, including *Meditation for Two*, which he wrote with photographer Keron Psillas and is also available from Trafalgar Square Books.

Dominique, along with his wife Debra and daughters Domina and Tianna, resides in Northern California in the Sonoma Valley. He spends much of his time now, when not teaching, in Brazil, where his association with Lusitano breeders has allowed him to undertake another of his life's passions: spreading the love of the Lusitano horse to riders around the world.

maria katsamanis

Dr. Maria Katsamanis is a horse trainer and clinician. She holds a doctorate in clinical psychology and has numerous publications in the area of psycho-physiology and breathing behavior. Her equine background is broad and includes working as a rider for a French racing barn. She maintains an academic appointment at Robert Wood Johnson Medical School and maintains her equine base in New Jersey.

Maria is part of a select few trainers outside of India who have worked with the rare Marwari horses.

Photos by Tom Chambers, courtesy of Francesca Kelly.

keron psillas

Keron Psillas was born in West Virginia in 1962 and has lived in Shepherdstown for most of her life. She was educated in local schools but says that her most meaningful education has come through observation and inquiry. As a lover of horses, of books, of art, people, mystery, and travel, Keron has crafted an emotionally and intellectually stimulating life by indulging these passions.

After more than 20 years as a parent and business owner, photography became an important creative outlet in 2004 while traveling in Scotland to research a book. As the photos became more an expression of an impression or feeling, rather than a documentary recording, it was apparent that the images were as important to the project as the writing.

In 2006, after a number of months living in Europe to focus solely on photography, Keron moved to Seattle and began two years tenure as the Director of the Art Wolfe Digital Photography Center. The access to industry professionals and renowned artists facilitated her developing career as a photographer, writer, and as an image-editing and publishing consultant.

While continuing to learn from and assist several masters of photography, including Sam Abell and Arthur Meyerson, Keron is now instructing and leading trips worldwide. She resides half the year in Portugal, home to her beloved Lusitano, and spends the rest of the year traveling to teach as well as learn from her students.

Keron leads tours in Portugal and other parts of the world, fulfills commissions, and pursues personal photography projects.

Index

Heart
    energy field of, 47–48, 54–55,
        81–82
    intention and, 32–33
    rhythms/rate, 29–30, 32–33, 86, 92
Heuschmann, Gerd, 58–59, 61
Histamine, 86
Horse/rider relationships
    direction and, 58
    emotions and, 35–42
    heart rhythm synchronicity, 29–30
    higher state of consciousness in,
        108–109
    as intermolecular exchange, 11–12
    mental contract in, 53–54
    mirroring in, 90
    neutral thinking role, 33–35
    perceptions of, 51
    rider goals in, 74
    in training, 19–20
Horses
    as conduit of enlightenment, 41–42
    misconceptions about, 25
Hyperflexion, 58–59

In the moment. *See* Being present
Influence at a distance, 50
In-hand work, 33–34, 63, 77
Innocence, 119
Instructors. *See* Teachers
Intellectual, vs. spiritual, 46–47
Intention
    awareness of, 67–69
    clarity of, 103–104
    in molecular change, 94
    potential of, 19, 131–132
    research regarding, 32–33
Introduction to ESP (Hashimoto), 29
Intuitive perception, 64

Joy, 54, 105–106, 119, 132
Judo, 63
Jumping, 60

Kindness, 82, 116

László, Ervin, 32, 50
Laying on of hands, 86–87
Learning
    by horses, 65–67. *See also* Training
    by riders, 24, 95–96, 118, 124–125

Lehrer, Paul M., 91
Libet, Benjamin, 69
Life's work, being present as, 118–119
Lightness
    as connection, 21
    energy's role in, 82–83
    French idea of, 2–4, 51
    goal of, 98
    head/neck position in, 57, 58–60
    as horse's nature, 21
    misconceptions about, 25
    molecular connection in, 17, 51, 57
    Molecular Mantra, 90
    new paradigm for, 16–18
    openness and, 129
    as state of mind, 21, 71, 99
Limitations, limiting of, 125, 128
Lipton, Bruce, 14
Longeing, 33–34, 41, 77
Love
    as choice, 96
    cultivating, 35–39
    education as, 74
    energy of, 82
    joy as product of, 105–106
    in oneness, 51
    in place of fear, 40–41
Lovelock, James, 29
Low and deep position, 58–59

Magnetic frequencies, 92
Masters, copying, 102
Meaning, 106
Meditation/meditative practice
    benefits of, 17, 91
    Golden Ball exercise, 92–94
    as means of being present, 116–118
    research regarding, 75, 77
Mental component, of riding. *See also*
    Being present
    effects on physical, 61–63, 112
    as focus of rider effort, 5, 124
    in molecular change, 90–92
    preparation role, 11
    rider discipline, 74, 99, 113, 118
    training role, 19–20
Mental contract, 53–54
Mental discipline, developing, 118
Mind-body connection, 14, 41–42,
    105–106, 117
Mindfulness, 34–35, 91–92, 99, 118, 119

the alchemy of lightness